IN THE SHADOW OF

Born in the Rio Grande Valley in 1944, Gregory G. Reck made his first visit to Mexico at the age of two weeks. It was followed by many others. After his family moved to Houston, Texas, he studied sociology and anthropology at the university there and received his B.A. degree in 1966. He went on to study cultural anthropology at the Catholic University of America, in Washington, D.C., earning his M.A. and Ph.D. degrees in 1968 and 1972. His Mexican anthropological work began with an analysis of a health-education project in Jonotla, the village in the eastern Sierra Madre Mountains that is also the background of the present book. Professor Reck has served as editorial assistant for the *Anthropological Quarterly* and has taught at the District of Columbia Teachers College, the University of Maryland, the Catholic University of America, and, since 1972, at Appalachian State University, in Boone, North Carolina.

Gregory G. Reck

IN THE SHADOW OF TLALOC
Life in a Mexican Village

WAVELAND
PRESS, INC.
Prospect Heights, Illinois

For information about this book, write or call:
Waveland Press, Inc.
P.O. Box 400
Prospect Heights, Illinois 60070
(708) 634-0081

Cover: Young *mestizo* boy—a close friend of the authors.

For Mae and my friends in Jonotla
who have given me more than
they can ever know

Contents

List of Illustrations

9

Acknowledgments

There are many individuals who have shared in various ways in the story that is told in these pages, and I would like to mention just a few of them. My awakening to the passion of anthropology I owe to Gilbert Kushner, whose critical mind and sensitive heart I hope are adequately reflected here. For guidance and support during my field research, I want to thank Michael Kenny, whose anthropological style has influenced me greatly. Also, I want to thank Regina Herzfeld and Conrad Reining for their contributions to my original field research and writing.

I want to thank my friend and colleague, Dan German, for his reading of parts of this manuscript and for his many contributions to the theoretical perspective on research which underlies this book. For assisting in the often thankless task of typing parts of the original manuscript, I want to thank Amy German and Teresa Trivette; and not enough can be said for my editor at Penguin Books, Susan Zuckerman, who was able to see what I was trying to say about anthropology and human beings and, thus, to edit with both precision and purpose.

A large measure of thanks goes to my family. My mother, Maria Heinecken Reck, and my father, George B. Reck, have both provided me with whatever sensitivity and writing ability might be reflected in these pages; my wife, Una Mae Lange Reck, assisted me in many invaluable ways during the original research and the often trying times of writing this manuscript. Finally, mention should be made of a little person who is probably unaware of her contribution to sustaining me, and thus this manuscript, over the past four years: our daughter, Nicolya Alexandra Reck.

Most of all, I want to thank the people who really are at

the heart of this book—the people of Jonotla, who tolerated and even supported me when they really had no reason to do so. This is particularly true of the three main characters of the book, to all of whom I have given pseudonyms. Despite cultural gulfs, we shared with one another our common human struggle, as they neatly carved away the facade of the roles of the anthropologist and his informants to reveal the persons beneath, teaching human lessons of an undefinable nature and an inestimable value. Such a gift does not demand repayment, and even if it did, there is no real way to make good the return.

Thanks to all of you.

Preface

For three months during the summer of 1967 and again for about ten months from September through the middle of June, 1969–1970, my wife and I carried out anthropological research in the remote east-central Mexican village of Jonotla. All of the research was a part of my advanced studies in cultural anthropology at the Catholic University of America. We came at a time of significant change for the village, which was then experiencing a considerable reduction in its isolation and independence from the outside world. As a consequence, we concentrated in our research on the process of change that was occurring and the repercussions of that change for village residents.

Jonotla, located in the rugged Sierra Norte of the state of Puebla, had a population of just over fifteen hundred people. Certain outside forces such as the construction of a road to the village in 1969, the governmental encouragement of the local growth of coffee, and the accompanying discouragement of traditional subsistence crops, as well as certain internal forces like population growth, inheritance patterns, and soil depletion, were leading to an intensification of the relationship between the village and the outside world. The people of Jonotla were, in a sense, experiencing for the first time the intrusion of those things which most of us readily associate with the modern twentieth century—roads, cars and buses, electricity, and a more competitive, individualistic way of life. It was our job to understand how this was happening and what it meant for the people who were living these changes.

This book concentrates on the experiences of a single individual and his struggle to adjust to the changes impinging on his small world. The events depicted took place between the fall of 1969 and the spring of 1970, but my understanding of them and the people involved started with my initial contact with the village in 1967 and runs through my last brief visit during the summer of 1976.

All the people in this book are real; I have used pseudonyms in order to protect their identities. Because they are real people and because I have shared an important part of life with them, I have made no pretense of complete objectivity. To the contrary, I have strained to maintain my subjectivity as well as theirs, as far as it was necessary to depict the passion of their lives. I cannot deny, nor do I even desire to, that at times I admired them and that at other times I was thoroughly disgusted with them. There were moments when I wanted to embrace them, and once or twice I did; in other situations I wanted to fight with them, and several times I came close. They generated fear, anger, love, disgust, pity, scorn, and admiration in me, and I am sure that at times I did in them as well. In short, they were always fully human, and I have tried to present them in that way, balancing accuracy with passion in the description of their lives as they were actually lived. Yet, as they appear here, there is no denying that they are partly a creation, for any attempt to understand another human being is a creative act born from the deepest human feelings that bind people together.

I was present during most of what is described in the chapters to follow, and what I did not directly experience was reported to me by the participants. In spite of this, I have removed myself from the story. This was not an easy decision, but in the end I felt that the material would have more impact and, in a sense, more truth, if it was presented in this way. By absenting myself from the story, I hope to bring to life for the reader a few individuals and their way of life—one that has existed for centuries, one that is fast disappearing.

Even though I have tried to maintain the human passions in my description of the lives that are depicted, and therefore have forgone a more traditional anthropological presentation, the reader would be well advised to keep in mind a cultural division that is important in understanding not only the impact of change on the village as a whole, but also the struggle to adapt on the part of the individuals who make up this story: the distinction between *indios* and *mestizos*. Jonotla, like many other villages in Mexico, is the home of two different cultures that have existed side by side for centuries. Originally, these two terms were part of a complex racial system established by the Spanish after the conquest, with *indio* referring to the native peoples with pure Indian ancestry and *mestizo* meaning individuals with one Spanish and one Indian parent. However, over the centuries the degree of population mixture has been so great that the biological meanings of the words have become meaningless. Today, instead of genetic background or physical appearance, these concepts classify individuals with essentially different cultural orientations. In other words, a *mestizo* and an *indio* do not necessarily look different from one another, but they do dress differently, speak differently, and behave differently.

The differences in language, clothing, and behavior between *indio* and *mestizo* are important, but more significant are the contrasting world views of the two groups. For the *indio*, life is essentially adjustment to what he perceives as the given order of things. He does not seek to dominate or control life, but instead attempts to come to harmonious or at least mutually tolerable terms with life. He considers himself to be a participant in the given order of the universe, drawing his strength and security not from personal victory and acclaim, but from the belief that in subjugating self-assertion, control, power, and wealth, he will have realized and accepted his human limits, and thus his nature.

For the *mestizo*, life is combat—with others and with oneself. Life does not *have* troubles; it *is* trouble. And to be alive is to race headlong into that trouble and into life. The *mestizo* does not attempt to accommodate himself to the world; rather, he defies it, challenges it, and fights with it. Life is seen as almost constant struggle, and although victories are the desired goals, even defeat is admired if it occurs with defiance and contempt for the victor. Life is a war which in the end will surely be lost, so that the most that one can expect are small victories over others and over the limits of one's own life.

These contrasting world views—the one unaggressive, accommodating, and group-oriented, and the other aggressive, competitive, and individualistic—can be seen in various areas of village life: in economic ideals, where the *indio* idealizes self-sufficient corn cultivation while the *mestizo* values more competitive commercial activities; in interpersonal relationships, where *indios* are generally reserved and passive and *mestizos* are most often highly aggressive, surrounded by the demands of *machismo*; in attitudes toward

Village scene

change, where the *indio* generally values the stability of tradition, while the *mestizo* values changes that allow him to
expand his control over people and things; and so on. This
indio world view and the behavior which is aligned with it
are born out of a synthesis of some elements of preconquest
Indian culture with elements developed and forced upon
them by subsequent Spanish and Mexican policies; the *mestizo* world view and its accompanying behavior have their
source in a multitude of postconquest factors, including in
the twentieth century, the Mexican Revolution and the mod-
ernization and industrialization of vast sectors of Mexico.

Although these differences that have only briefly been
dealt with here are generalizations, and like all such statements tend to oversimplify and mask the complexity which
underlies human motivations and actions, they nevertheless
are important in fully understanding the struggle depicted in
this book. The village of Jonotla, inhabited by both *indios*
and *mestizos,* is not only experiencing changes that are opening it up to the outside world, but also changes that are removing the psychological, cultural, and economic supports
for the *indio* world view. As a result, *indios* are in fact becoming *metizos* in their dress, their language, their behavior, and their view of life. The central personality in this
book is in the midst of such a transition. Born an *indio*, he
now finds himself in a *mestizo* world which he does not
fully understand or fully desire.

Finally, it is not my intention to turn this story into a
struggle between good (tradition, *indios*) and evil (change,
mestizos). Such a simple distinction would suppose that I
understood the true nature of life and would only obscure
the passion which is at the heart of every human story. But
this book is about conflict, about the struggle between
past and future, and, most important, the struggle with oneself. As such, it is about the struggle, the joy, the love, and
the pain that we call life.

My journey was done, and behind me lay hill and dale, and Life and Death. How shall man measure Progress there where the dark-faced Josie lies? How many heartfuls of sorrow shall balance a bushel of wheat? How hard a thing is life to the lowly, and yet how human and real. And all this life and love and strife and failure, is it the twilight of nightfall or the flush of some faint-dawning day?

—W. E. B. DUBOIS,
The Souls of Black Folk

In the Shadow
of Tlaloc

1-Some Worlds

Some worlds are straight and flat,
continuous stretches of sameness,
seemingly unaware of the strengths
and mysteries which formed them.
Others are crooked and cragged,
voluptuous images of mystery and
age, seemingly proud to display
the multiple and sometimes strange
faces of nature. The sun rises
and sets on both worlds, beaming
and laughing its way into night,
and alone knowing which world will
surrender to the other.

It was the late winter of the year 12-Reed.* The early morning mist and fog danced in circles just beyond the reach of the campfires, the warm orange and yellow flames striking out in vain against the cold dampness that had settled during the night. A few dim figures wrapped heavily in cloaks were beginning to stir about while others struggled against the morning for a few more moments of rest on the hard ground. The early greeting songs of birds were beginning to

---

* A.D. 1180 This account is based primarily on a combination of local histories given by two village residents and the writings of José Garcia Rayón, a recorder of early Spanish history in Mexico (*Descripción del Pueblo de Gueytlalpan, 30 de Mayo, 1581*). It should not be read as literal history.

filter through the fog, assuring those who were already up and about that there was still a recognizable world out there beyond the limited range of their vision.

This was the beginning of another day, more uncomfortable than most, but not unlike the countless others that had preceded it. No one there yet knew that it was also the dawning of the day for which they had long hoped and waited, expending the energy from their bodies, minds, and souls. The fog concealed more than they knew.

Years earlier, they had uprooted themselves from the only home that any of them had ever known in order to go in search of a sacred sign that their gods had promised awaited them. They had wandered with the faith of children, not knowing what the sign would be but confident that they would know it when it finally did come. And wherever that sign would appear, they knew that they would build their new home. It was their own particular vision and sense of destiny which kept them searching, but they were urged on by the same hopes and fears that had moved countless others to search for a new day in a promised land.

With this faith in their gods and in themselves, they had left a land of rugged, parched mountains where signs of human life were almost as rare as the rainfall which was eagerly swallowed by the dry, cracked soil on which it fell. It was a harsh land where even the plants seemed poised in ready defense against external enemies. The scant rainfall seemed to force life inward, as each small patch of thorned bush, each group of tall, prickly cacti were like small islands, separated from the next nearest isle by a gulf of dust and rock. Even when the welcome rains did finally come, they often seemed unfriendly, coming in sudden bursts of fury, transforming the dusty arroyos into short-lived raging streams which carved ever deeper into the ancient rock.

And, yet, it was a land that they had found difficult to leave. For despite the many trials of a tenuous existence, based on a diet of widely scattered wild plants and small game, they had come to know their small world well. It provided them with a sort of security that in many ways over-shadowed the problem of wresting a living from a harsh land. It was an indication of the power of their vision that they had been willing to foresake this security for an uncertain future in an unknown land.

During their journey they had seen landscapes which they had not known existed. The face of the land they had crossed was marked by both the ravages and the beauty of old age, unveiling the hints of times and experiences which they as humans could never know. Mountains were everywhere, the backbone of the land. But even so, the mountains had many expressions, from the nearly barren peaks that they had left to the central highland with broad mile-high plateaus fringed by pine-covered slopes, to snow covered volcanic summits like the twin peaks of Popocatepetl and Iztaccihuatl, and into the dense greenness of the eastern escarpment in which they now were camped. The lands that they had crossed were living testimony to the multiple and sometimes unfathomable faces of nature; each one seemed to harbor its own world with is own particular variations in rainfall, temperatures, vegetation, winds, and soil. They had been at different times entranced, surprised, and overwhelmed by it all, and now they were near exhaustion.

This morning they found themselves once again in an unfamiliar land, and in some ways a disagreeable one—cool, damp, and covered with thick vegetation that made it difficult to travel. They had reached the eastern edge of the massive pyramid of mountains that covered the bulk of the land. Beyond them, to the east, the mountains dropped rather suddenly into the broad coastal lowland. The rain-filled clouds blowing in from the ocean across the damp coast would frequently collide with and envelope these mountains for days at a time, releasing their moisture and depriving the lands farther west of life-giving rain. Like almost everything in their world, it was fateful circumstance and mystery which shaped the face of this land and the others that they had crossed.

Certainly, it was not the mountains which made them feel like strangers. They had never really known anything else. But these were somehow different—green instead of brown, thickly clad instead of naked, soft-skinned instead of rock-hard, full instead of empty. All about them, these strange green mountains swooped skyward out of narrow, deep valleys cut by water and time. Giant boulders jutted abruptly from the soft, lush skin of the earth, revealing small entrances to the world beneath. Rivers and numerous smaller streams alternately meandered and roared in their journey to the eastern coastal plain and the vast ocean beyond. And the vegetation, nourished by the year-round rainfall, expanded into every available corner of the earth.

As strange lands most often do, this one made them uneasy, both physically and mentally. But it was a discomfort made tolerable by their faith in things to come. As a result, the strangeness of the present became suspended in time between the memories of the past and the hope of the future. And so they pushed on, vigilant in their search for that sacred sign.

The morning was quickly warming, dissipating the fog at higher elevations. A vague blueness, like a desert mirage, was beginning to appear above their heads through the swirls of fog. Soon it would be a clear, warm day, more to their liking. From their camp alongside a small stream running through a grassy knoll, they could see a few mountaintops emerging above the fog which seemed to be increasingly sucked down into the deep valleys. Rising as they did above the soft, dense fog, the peaks appeared to be floating in a vast white sea. More and more people were awakening, and the camp was beginning to take on the familiar sights and sounds of morning routines.

In one high corner of the camp, a tall, lean man stood silently looking out over the gradually clearing skies. More than any other among them, he had expended his recent life energies in the search for their new home. His name was

Ixoceolotl,* which meant Ocelot Face, a recognition of both the sanctity and power of his position as their leader. He was a warrior and a priest as well. As a great warrior and a person who stood in a special relationship with the gods, he received the rewards of his position—wealth, servants, power. But he also felt the burdens of responsibility for his people, a responsibility to lead them to their destiny. He had always managed to lead them with silent strength on their journey with no known destination, a fact that had held' them together during difficult times. But now even he was growing tired.

Ixoceolotl watched the mountains emerge from the fog with few expectations; his gaze searched for nothing, for it was numbed and blurred by his thoughts. Yet, out there near the limits of his vision, his gaze and his thoughts seemed slowly to pull something strange from the roof of the fog. Although it was only several miles directly in his line of vision, he did not seem immediately to notice it. Slowly his eyes focused on the strange sight as they strained for some additional sign that would help him to identify what he was seeing. There against a background of higher mountain peaks was what appeared to be a long level ridge with some sort of rectangular structure standing at its center.

Calling some of his close aides together, Ixoceolotl discussed the possibilities with them. By now, everyone was staring toward the ridge and a quiet curiosity and excitement was stirring throughout the camp. Most believed that the ridge cradled a Totonac village and that the large structure was a temple of some sort. They knew that they were not too far southwest of the great Totonac holy place called Tajin and that they had already entered land that was inhabited by these east-coast dwellers. If it was a Totonac settlement, they knew that they would be viewed as invaders, which in a very real sense they were. For nothing, not even

---

* Also spelled Ixoxolotl.

the shedding of their own and others' blood would stand in their way.

Ixoceolotl was almost alone in his disagreement with the others, for he believed, or perhaps only hoped, that they had finally found the sign for which they had long searched. His feelings prevailed, and it was decided that several of the fleetest and bravest warriors would be sent to the ridge to find out the nature of the peculiar formation that sat atop it. The ridge was several hours' walk away over rough terrain, but the men were given only until midmorning, when the sun would be at its greatest height, to return with some word. If they failed to hear from them by that time, more warriors would be sent to the ridge.

The entire camp waited throughout the morning, suspending their routine activities until the men returned. Some of the warriors, anticipating the worst, prepared themselves for battle. Ixoccolotl stared at the ridge in silence.

By midmorning, the now blazing sun had burned away most of the fog from the face of the land, revealing the deep colors of the earth and the clear morning sky. In the distance, the ridge filtered through a lingering thin haze, giving it a greenish-blue hue which seemed to link the colors of the earth with that of the heavens. The ridge seemed so distant and yet so close, shimmering like an oasis mirage in a desert.

As midday approached, the envoys returned, and people crowded about them to find out what they had discovered. But the men refused to report anything except to Ixoceolotl directly. They spoke with him alone for what seemed a very long time, until finally he turned toward the people and spoke firmly to them: "We are going to the mountain; it is the sign." He said no more, and his people understood, for this day had been a long time in coming. They had left their home to wander across strange lands and confront strange peoples; they had fought battles and made uneasy alliances with these peoples; they had become sick from unfamiliar food and weather; many of them had died in places far from their home and been buried there like strangers. Now, finally, they had arrived. Their gods had spoken the truth. Their faith had been justified.

They traveled as quickly as they could over the rough terrain toward the ridge, watching the sign momentarily disappear behind the mountains as they stumbled downward into deep narrow valleys, only to have it reappear, closer and larger, as they reached the next summit. Each time that they descended into a gorge or ravine and were faced with the task of struggling out once again, it was as if the sign that was now indelibly imprinted in their minds pulled them upward, to the top where that image was once again merged with that real vision before their eyes. Closer and closer they came until after several hours they stood exhausted at the base of the ridge.

A thousand feet above them stood the formation which many still thought to be some sort of human construction —a tall, rectangular stone structure. They made the final ascent up the more gradually sloping south end of the ridge. It was an arduous climb, made even more difficult by the thick foliage that blocked every line of possible ascent. But soon the ground started to level out, and they knew that they were near the top and would soon see for themselves what Ixoceolotl had so confidently proclaimed to be the sign from their gods. There was a momentary hesitation in their movement, arising from the brief fear of unfulfilled expectations. They had wandered so long and so hard for this moment, and now that it was irrevocably upon them, they feared the worst—that they had done all of this for nothing. There was a feeling of disbelief, doubt, betrayal, and, most of all, fear. But it passed quickly.

As they cleared a group of trees located at the narrow tip of the southern end of the ridge, the sign they sought loomed a hundred yards directly in front of them. It was not a stone structure, but a rock formation. It was not a human construction, but a creation of the gods. The steel-gray bare rock shot a hundred feet skyward from the ridge,

its sides almost perfectly straight and its top apparently
flat, as if it had been placed there in some whimsical moment by nature. But Ixoceolotl and his followers were certain that the intentions of the gods were anything but fanciful. For them, the rock was a sacred sign of incredible
beauty and obvious solemnity. In their long journey, they
had encountered numerous peoples who had spent many
years of difficult labor constructing massive earth and stone
pyramids, man-made mountains with flat platforms on top
from which the people could reach upward toward their
gods. They had been awed by these structures and by the
people who built them. The pyramids were impressive testimony to the importance of the gods to those who constructed them. But now the long ridge upon which they
stood rose like an immense thousand-foot pyramid above
two snake-like rivers, crowned with this magnificent hun-
dred-foot temple platform, testimony of their importance
as people to the gods. Without doubt, they were truly a
chosen people.

Up to this moment, they had been known only as Chichimecs, or Sons of Dogs, as uncivilized foragers who lacked
the artistic, architectural, political, religious, and military
skills of the agricultural city builders who populated the central highlands. Although they had learned many of the skills
of the agriculturalists and adopted elements of their culture, including many of their gods, they had always remained Chichimecs—savage nomads of the arid north. As
a small part of a massive movement of various Chichimec
peoples southward, they were unknowingly playing a small
part in the transformation of the human face of the land.
The old cities and ceremonial centers were giving way to
new ones as the centers of power that had long been established were slowly eroded. Farther to the west, another
Chichimec group calling themselves Colhua Mexica, or Aztec, were still pursuing the sacred sign that had been promised by their gods and accumulating the knowledge and
strength that would soon make them known and feared

throughout the land. But even if Ixoceolotl and his people had known of these events, they would not, for the moment, have cared. For now the universe revolved around them—a chosen people in the promised land.

Ixoceolotl named the sacred rock Tlaloctepetl, the mountain of Tlaloc, the god who, he believed, had led them here. Tlaloc was a god who had been borrowed from the agriculturalists. He was the god of rain and, thus, the very god of life to tillers of the soil: "He who makes plants spring up." In this sense, he was largely a beneficent god existing in a pantheon of often terrifying and vindictive deities. Those who were fortunate enough to go and live with Tlaloc after their death lived forever in a fertile idyllic garden with an eternal supply of corn, beans, chilis, and squash. Those who were fortunate to receive his favors while on earth were guaranteed an abundant—but somewhat less than eternal—supply of these same necessary and valued goods of life. Such was the hoped-for fate of Ixoceolotl and his people, both in this life and the next.

They built their village on the north slope of the ridge not too far from the sacred rock of Tlaloc. The village was called Xonotl, after a tree that grew in abundance there and was believed to possess medicinal properties. Using their new skills as agriculturalists, they settled down to village life, cultivating corn, beans, and squash, the sacred diet that they had adopted since moving southward. And they used their new religious skills to persuade Tlaloc to rain his life-giving semen down upon their fields.

The sacred rock, Tlaloctepetl, was the center of their life. There the priests would carefully climb the northern face of the rock to what seemed to be the very roof of this world. The top of the rock was a completely level area of some hundred square yards, a perfectly formed platform from which they had a sweeping view of both the land, which depended upon the benevolence of Tlaloc, and the heavens, which cradled his realm far beyond the senses of living men. There they would make their pleas for rain or give their thanks

The sacred rock Tlaloctepetl

for rain already given, sometimes carving out the hearts of sacrificial victims to emphasize their sincerity and faith. Despite the steep slopes and often thin soil, the heavy rains from Tlaloc made the land a veritable Eden for them, and they were well pleased with their fate.

Like all visionaries who leave their homes in search of a promised land, the people who founded the village of Xonotl were obsessed by their destiny. Convinced that the deities held a special place for them in their hearts as well as on earth, they believed in the immortality and invincibility of themselves as a people. When the promised land was finally theirs, a stable and enduring world was envisioned for the future, in sharp contrast to the instability that had severed them from their original home and accompanied them on their journey. There was no need for change in a promised land, no need for dreams or hopes, since all had been fulfilled. Visions of change were vanquished from their minds, for the gods had taken them to their bosoms and it was impossible to conceive that anyone would want to leave the warmth and security of that place.

Ixoceolotl and his people, believing that they had found the promised land, envisioned a timeless era of continuity, stretching out over the vast face of the future, blurring the distinction between now and then. But they could not foretell what awaited their descendants in the realm of Tlaloc. New visions of promised lands held by newly chosen peoples supplanted their own. First came their former Chichimec kinsmen, the Aztecs, fighting a holy war in support of the Sun against the forces of darkness and destruction and subjugating the descendants of Ixoceolotl to that end through the forced payment of tribute and the spilling of sacrificial blood. Shortly afterward came another people with yet another vision of the promised land—gold, land, and wealth. The Spanish once again harnessed the lives of the people of Xonotl—now renamed Jonotla by the new lords of the land—and the promised land of Ixoceolotl became little more than a prison with few means of escape. Over the centuries, Utopian visions came and went like the winter fogs, testimony to the instability of a world once thought to be so permanent.

Yet, through all of this, some things remained as they had been on that now distant day in the year 12-Reed when Tlaloc reached out through the fog to Ixoceolotl and his people. The ancient mountains erupting from the land remained; the same rivers and streams washed through familiar valleys; the morning songs of birds still greeted those close enough to hear; the winter mist and fog still shrouded the land in discomfort; the hard summer rains endured; and Tlaloctepetl still looked out over the vast expanse of heaven and earth. But the promised land that had been discovered on that day was no more. The vision of Ixoceolotl, born out of the destruction of the past, the lingering memories of what once was, and the hopeful dreams of what might forever be, had failed to create the realm of Tlaloc in this land. Today, all that remains of that dream is a world vaguely tied to the past by frayed cultural threads and common human passions, a world set in the shadow of Tlaloc.

2–Sounds of the World to Come

As evening comes, the river rhythm
echoes through the hills, awakening
the mountain melodies. Small
life listens and dances to the familiar
sounds of the global harmony. The
welcome music resonates through the air
slowly settling over every rock and
tree, a quilt of sound laid gently over
the evening earth. Until with the
coming of the new sun, all falls silent
and the mountains sleep, awaiting the
sounds of the world to come.

Slowly the full silence of the mountain night, broken only occasionally by the whisper of small, hidden animal life, was giving way to the morning sounds coming from the village of Jonotla. Each and every night seemed to belong to the mountains, as the world of humans fell silent soon after the sun sat for one last long moment atop the western peaks, sending a farewell of brilliant colors into the sky before disappearing into the blackness. But if the nights belonged to the mountains, as they had for millions of years before the coming of men, then the days were now possessed by a human world. Each new morning, as the first light flickered over the peaks to the east, the white-plastered, red-roofed village houses that spread out beneath the rock of Tlaloc slowly emerged from the massive green of the mountains. The first muffled sounds of babies crying, young children chattering to their weary parents, burros lazily clumping along the cobblestoned streets, roosters crowing sharp and shrill, dogs barking at the disappearing night, and womens' hands rhythmically pounding cornmeal into the day's food rose slowly to greet the sun at the brim of the mountain. It was as if the gradually rising intensity of the village sounds gently coaxed the sun to show its bright face, until, together, sound and sun created the day.

It was December 12, 1969. For a winter day, the morning was already unusually warm. The village had for six previous days been shrouded in a cloak of fog and cold. But even had the warm sun not broken through the dense fog which had for so long separated it from the mountains below, men would today have had good reason for celebration, for this was no ordinary day. It was the Day of our Lady of Guadalupe, a fiesta day celebrating the moment when the Virgin of Guadalupe had first appeared to the *indio* Juan Diego near Mexico City in 1531. Her extraordinary appearance had led to the conversion of millions of *indios* to Catholicism, thus establishing one of the most significant national fiestas of all.

According to the story, a beautifully clothed *indio* woman, who identified herself as the Mother of God, had appeared to Diego on the hill of Tepeyac, which had earlier been associated with the Aztec earth-and-fertility goddess, Tonantzin, and requested that a church be built on top of the hill to commemorate Her. Although Diego's story was initially greeted with a great deal of skepticism by the newly established Catholic hierarchy in Mexico City, the third time that She appeared the evidence was sufficiently convincing. She told Diego to collect a bouquet of wild flowers to give to the doubters, and when he removed the flowers from the cape in which he carried them, there was an imprint of the Virgin inside it, a sign to the Catholic hierarchy, as well as to the recently conquered *indios* of Mexico, that the reported miracle was real. Thus the indigenous mother goddess Tonantzin was merged with the Christian Virgin. The event symbolized the moment when one historical period disappeared forever into the shape of a new age, and its commemoration that day symbolized the time when the steady, often difficult trip through life to death yielded to the hope of momentary transcendence.

The village had been in preparation for weeks. Men had decreased their labors in the fields and increased their drinking in the bars; women had been busy decorating household altars and preparing such special foods as *tamales* and *atole*; schoolchildren delightedly listened to the story of the remarkable encounter between Diego and the Virgin. The *mayordomo* was the person responsible for organizing and paying for the traditional aspects of the fiesta. For weeks he, too, had been busy organizing people and events, soliciting funds from relatives, and buying the various items re-

Village street

quired for any worthwhile fiesta. Indeed, for the very first
time, a carnival with rides and games of chance was crawl-
ing up the newly built road that scarred the side of the
mountain leading to the village. In short, the gradual dis-
appearance of ordinary routines and their replacement by
the unusual and special noticeably transformed the charac-
ter of the village.

But if the fiesta had preoccupied most villagers' minds,
there was at least one person for whom such concerns
seemed remote. He sat alone in a darkened room in his
house, not thinking of the fiesta, but reading in a thick illustrated dictionary. Periodically he would lift his reluctant
five-foot-three-inch frame from the chair and walk slowly
around the room, trying to stretch the sleep from his bones.
His face was plump and round, making his head appear
slightly too large for his small body. A small-brimmed straw
hat was pushed toward the back of his head, still shading
his narrow dark eyes and the thin wisp of hair above his
mouth. His light-blue shirt pulled apart at the buttons, and
the top button on his tan pants would not close, evidence of
a recent increase in weight. All in all, his plump face and
slightly pudgy body made him look boyish, belying his
thirty years.

He had been awake since the first rays of the sun had cast
a subtle light on the village, sending a crack of day through
the shutter in the room where he, his wife, and three-year-
old daughter slept on a single bed. He did not particularly
want to be awake, for on this fiesta day he did not have to
go to the fields where he worked as a hired laborer. But the
incessant crowing of the old rooster that patrolled the
street outside had forced his awakening. He wondered how
his wife and daughter were managing to remain asleep. But
then it was not often that they missed the beginning of
each new day.

Fatigue clouded his eyes and mind, so that he was only
partially aware that his lips were moving. He was mouthing
the words, "Gothic; a style of architecture characterized by

the converging of weights and strains at isolated points."
Printed next to the definition was an illustration of some
obscure European cathedral. He nodded his head approv-
ingly, and his knitted eyebrows revealed the strain of his
attempt to memorize the totally alien concept. Of course,
he had no idea when he would have the opportunity to let
it be known that he understood the meaning of the word
Gothic. But this way, just in case the chance did arise, he
would be prepared. Should the conversation tomorrow in
the fields happen to turn to cathedrals, or Europe, or architecture, or even weights and strains, he would get the
chance to drop his small but impressive bombshell.

After all, had not he—Celistino de la Cruz—already
gained countless valuable bits of information from the dictionary? He had learned, for instance, that North America
was connected to Mexico and that one did not have to
travel by boat to get there, as he had once thought. He had
learned that some forms of rhinoceros have only one horn,
while others have two. And he was probably the only person
within a hundred miles who knew what a clavichord was.
Hadn't he already stopped numerous conversations dead in
their tracks with such gems of knowledge? Hadn't he turned
countless heads, dropped many a chin, and raised numerous
eyebrows with his comments on various unusual subjects?
He was convinced that his knowledge of such things would
eventually help him acquire what he desired—a store and a
good reputation, so that people would respect him and his
opinions. He wanted people to say to themselves when faced
with an important decision or a need for information, "I
will go ask Celistino de la Cruz. He will surely know." And
who could say? It might just be the word "Gothic" that
would be the key.

He had received the dictionary from a medical student
who, like all future doctors in Mexico, was required to complete an internship in a community that lacked adequate
health care. The intern's office had been on the first floor
of the house in which Celistino and his family lived in a

A *first-generation* mestizo *family*

rented room. They had spent many an enjoyable hour together, discussing such things as goiters and suppositories, and Celistino had developed an authentic admiration for the young city doctor. Celistino found his knowledge increasingly admirable. Before the intern left to establish a permanent practice elsewhere, he gave Celistino a box of medicine, a pharmaceutical encyclopedia, a pregnancy calendar, and the dictionary. Such was the legacy left by one of Celistino's true heroes, a man who was successful in the terms of a world that Celistino was struggling to make his own.

Celistino had kept these Promethean gifts, thinking they might be useful if he ever decided to go into the curing business. Of course, he would never become a *curandero* who cures only with herbs and spells because he had learned about the flu, parasites, injections, pills, and suppositories from a bona fide doctor. But after seeing a real doctor practice, he knew deep down that he would never be able to diagnose and cure illness. So he planned to sell the medicine and most of the other things to one of the local schoolteachers who also practiced medicine on the side. He would never sell the dictionary, of course, for it was sure to be one of the keys to his eventual success. So whenever possible, he read in the dictionary, even on the Day of Our Lady of Guadalupe.

In contrast, all the preparation and anticipation for this day was nowhere more evident than at the house of Abelardo Perez de Gaona, the *mayordomo* of the fiesta. Don Abelardo had begun to prepare for this day almost thirty years ago, when as a young man he had prayed and made a *promesa*, a sacred promissory exchange, to the Virgin in order to solicit Her aid in fighting the illness that plagued his first child. It had been perfectly reasonable that he turn to the Virgin, for She had spoken these words to Juan Diego in 1531:

I may show and make known and give all my love, my mercy, and my help and my protection—I am in truth your merciful mother—to you and to all the other people dear to me.

And even though don Abelardo rarely accompanied his wife and children to Mass, he still was a *cristiano* just as certainly as he was a man.

So sick had his young daughter been that she had not willingly eaten for two weeks, and most of the time she had lain motionless in her mother's arms. Finally, don Abelardo took three candles, a bouquet of wild flowers gathered from the edge of his cornfield, twenty *centavos*, and a sad resignation to the Chapel of the Little Virgin outside the village. The chapel was built on a spot where a local version of that 1531 miracle had occurred. In 1922 the Virgin had appeared to a small *indio* boy and, as proof of Her appearance, left a five-inch-long impression of Herself carved in a rock, the rock once known as Tlaloctepetl. This stimulated much religious excitement and fervor in the village. A small chapel had been partially constructed on the site, but because it lacked the sanction of the Catholic hierarchy, it had never been completed. Nevertheless, the half-finished chapel was thought by most to be the home of the Little Virgin. Despite what he knew to be the love of the Virgin, don Abelardo had not been hopeful She could help him. After all, he was only one troubled man among countless others, and even if the Virgin were to take note of his plight, the final expression of Her love might not be what he was hoping for—the life of his child.

But suppressing his doubts he had given his small offerings and asked for Her aid, and, almost as an afterthought, promised to sponsor Her fiesta if his daughter lived. For another week, he and his wife waited with their child, forcing her to eat and drink whenever they could. Don Abelardo's wife did not share his pessimism, for as she later put it, "the Virgin knows the suffering of a mother for her child." Many times, especially over the preceding weeks, she had stopped in the church to look at the statue of the Virgin. A path of tears flowed from Her incredibly pained expression to the casket encasing a statue of the crucified Christ which lay at Her feet. How could She not understand and have compassion for the suffering of a woman and mother here on earth?

Somehow, miraculously, their daughter's eyes had gradually brightened and her small arms and legs once again started to kick energetically. And so don Abelardo and his wife remembered their *promesa*. Almost thirty years later, they were repaying their debt.

Sitting in his house in the early morning hours, watching and smiling at the gaiety that surrounded him, he thought of how little he was actually going to repay the Virgin for the mercy that She had shown for such a young *campesino*. She was receiving a fiesta—not even a very expensive one since he had spent only about two thousand *pesos,* or what amounted to a little more than half of the yearly value of his agricultural labors—and in return he had gained a fine, strong daughter who had brought him a good, hardworking son-in-law and four beautiful grandchildren. There was little doubt in his mind that he had received infinitely more than he was now giving. But he was only a poor *campesino,* a small farmer, and the Virgin, he was certain, would understand.

The new morning sun filtered through the two windows and the open front door in don Abelardo's stone house. Several candles, which had provided light for the celebration that had begun around sundown the preceding day, blinked weakly in an apparent struggle with the sun to light the room. A small table had been fashioned into an altar by the addition of a white tablecloth, several strands of yellow and blue crepe paper, and various statues and pictures of the Virgin, Christ, and St. John the Baptist, the village patron saint. Scattered around the room were several chairs, most of which had been borrowed from relatives and neighbors. In one corner of the single room that, along with a small cooking area, formed the entire house, several children lay sleeping on the only bed and on several straw mats on the cement floor. They had somehow managed to fall alseep amidst all the celebration.

About fifteen men and women stood about the room, talking, laughing, and drinking. This was one of the few occasions when women could drink alcoholic beverages in public, although most of them still preferred to abstain. In the cooking area, several women busied themselves with the morning meal of tortillas, beans, and coffee. The group had already consumed dozens of tamales and several cases of soft drinks and beer and several liters of *refino.*

The night had been a full one, as it should have been, for it was a celebration of an event that occurs with this particular intersection of people but once in a lifetime. The existence of the fiesta was guaranteed forever by tradition as one of the few certainties in an uncertain life, although the

people would come and go. The Day of Our Lady of Guadalupe would come next year and the year after and the
year after that, but it would never again be sponsored by
don Abelardo; nor would all these same people ever again
be gathered together to help him celebrate what had happened thirty years earlier. There had been hours of incessant praying, dancing, singing, eating, laughing, drinking, and
speechmaking. Everyone seemed exhausted now. Everyone
except Los Negros.

Ten men would soon complete their transformation into
the traditional symbolic personification of the fiesta by
donning their costumes and assuming the identity of Los
Negros, the Black Ones. Unlike other celebrants who had
expended their energies in a flurry of excessiveness, the
ten dancers seemed slowly to gain momentum with the gradual coming of the morning. They understood that their roles
were transitory, but they were also aware that the meaning
of Los Negros far transcended them. For Los Negros had
the age of centuries and the weight of tradition, while they
were only mortal men whose existence was momentary and
insignificant.

No one really knew when the tradition of these dancers
had originated in Jonotla, but everyone knew that it was
quite impossible to conceive of this major fiesta without
Los Negros, or to conceive of Los Negros performing outside the context of the fiesta. They were inseparable and
essential to one another. The fiesta was a welcome break
in man's journey to an inevitable destination, a few days
during which time ceased moving in the only direction that
it knows, a brief moment in which the world stopped, allowing men to transcend themselves. Los Negros epitomized
this phenomenon. They represented ordinary men in their
extraordinary being. Their elaborate, somewhat whimsical
costumes did not make them special men, instead it made
men something special. They mirrored what every person
knew, or hoped, was reservoired in his soul. They were
Everyman's spirit.

As ordinary men they labored in the fields, in soiled white garments and ordinary straw hats, working with *asodones,* or digging sticks and heavy, rusty *machetes.* As *Los Negros* they wore shiny, bejeweled black satin and stiff black *sombreros* crowned with flowers. With colorful silk scarves, crepe paper, and castanets, they danced their labors to the joyful music of flute, fiddle, and guitar. The men had been selected as had been customary for years. Two of them were kinsmen of the *mayordomo;* two were his *compadres,* godfathers of his children; one was a close friend; and the remaining five were experienced dancers who had taught the dance steps and their meanings to the others. In addition, three musicians accompanied the dancers.

The dancers were not paid. They were, however, the primary beneficiaries of the rewards, both material and emotional, of the fiesta. The *mayordomo* had provided them with several full days of food and drink, and their cumulative emotional involvement in the role that carried such historical and symbolic weight was about to reach a crescendo. This was all the pay any man could desire.

The arrival of the morning sun from its night journey was the signal for the men to begin their final preparations. After eating lightly of tortillas and beans and drinking the thick black coffee made from the beans of the *criollo de la sierra,* a coffee plant that is especially adapted to the climate of the mountains, the men went outside onto the porch and changed into the dress of *Los Negros.* They were not solemn about the transition that they were about to complete, nor would a solemn attitude have helped them in any way. They were simply filled with the fiesta, quietly gay, and intermittently joking with one another.

Over their white cotton *pantalones,* traditionally worn by *indios,* they pulled up black-satin pants emblazoned with glittering multicolored sequins. Their shiny black-satin shirts were decorated with sequined flowers and birds dancing around the yokes. Silk scarves were tied around their waists and necks and fitted securely on their heads were black *sombreros* piled amusingly high with plastic flowers, small mirrors, and images of saints. The final touch was, for several of the men, more painful: they replaced their *huaraches*, the traditional sandals fashioned from rubber and leather thongs, with ankle-high black leather boots. Several of the men had never before worn shoes of any kind. Some of them had stored their shoes away in a closet or box and would only take them out for special occasions such as the visit of the national census taker. For various reasons, it might be to one's advantage to communicate to the national government that one did, indeed, wear shoes. The unbinding *huaraches* had allowed their feet full freedom to flatten out in such a way that they appeared to be almost perfect squares, as wide as they were long. For a few agonizing moments, the men grunted and cursed as they tried to put feet used to freedom into the confining shoe leather. And in those moments the back porch of don Abelardo's house was the scene of a strange contrast: men in the ancient, sacred role of *Los Negros* were being painfully reduced to mere mortals by the leather boots, a symbol of the modern world, encased tightly around their feet. The emotional edge that had been sharpened over the last few days seemed hopelessly dulled as several of them tiptoed back and forth on the porch, their grimacing faces muttering inaudible expressions in the names of their mothers and various saints and deities. The few men who were more accustomed to wearing shoes laughed and joked about their friends' plight.

"Look," one said, "their feet are more important to them than their souls!"

"Look at him kick and prance," another shouted out. "He looks just like a young burro the first time he is shoed!" And they laughed with delight, prodded on, no doubt, by their full bellies, the liters of *refino* that they had drunk over the past days, the headiness that followed sleepless nights, and their heightened anticipation of the day. Then, suddenly the gaiety disappeared as quickly as it had arrived as some of the men started to practice the rhythmic, stomping steps that characterized *Los Negros*. Finally don Emiliano, who had been one of the *Los Negros* dancers many times during the past twenty years, went inside the house and walked over to an elderly man who was sitting in a chair, silently taking long draws from a crumpled cigarette.

"We are ready, don Francisco," he said softly to the old man. Looking briefly at don Emiliano, the old man returned silently to the more essential task of finishing the cigarette before it fell apart in his hands. After a few more puffs, he extinguished it on the cement floor and picked bits of tobacco from his mouth. Then, smiling and nodding to don Emiliano, he picked up a small woven bag from the back of the chair and walked out into the bright sunlight.

Squinting from the sudden brightness, don Francisco casually surveyed all of the men. He glanced back and forth

Los Negros *dancers on the Day of our Lady of Guadalupe*

without even moving his head, although his thoughts were reflected in his wrinkled brow. Slowly his head sunk on his chest, and he laughed softly to himself. His thoughts were his alone, but he may have been thinking that it would not be easy to help transform such a motley, inexperienced crew into the symbolic transcendence that is *Los Negros*. He shrugged his shoulders helplessly and walked, bent and crooked, out to the cement patio behind the house. In just a few weeks, the patio would be covered with coffee beans from don Abelardo's coffee trees, drying in the late winter sun. Today the patio was serving a greater purpose.

Turning to the men, who had by now assembled themselves facing him and the distant mountains beyond, don Francisco scratched his short, ragged white beard and mop of dense, graying hair. His casual movements contrasted with the severe expressions on the faces of *Los Negros*. Don Francisco reached into the small bag, fumbling momentarily with its contents, and then quickly drew out a bundle of chicken feathers. Brushing some dirt from the feathers, he impatiently motioned for the men to move closer.

By now the sun was well on its way in its journey across the sky. Glancing up at its brightness, don Francisco pushed his straw hat down until it rested securely on his thick, projecting eyebrows. Certainly the sun was good and necessary, being an essential part of the unity that sustains all life, but in the brightness and the heat of midmorning, it seemed like too much of a good thing. Under the sun's warm gaze, one by one, the men approached don Francisco, and in the infant morning he hurriedly brushed the entire body of each one, taking a new feather each time. He muttered the same words over and over: "Our Lady of Guadalupe, Queen of Mexico, Mother of us all, remove the sins from this man that he may receive you."

Most of the people who had been inside the house were now standing on the back porch, arms folded, watching intently the scene on the patio. When he had completed this ritual with each of the men, don Francisco called out a name, and a young boy who had been watching from the porch ran over, took the feathers, and along with some old newspapers burned them. With this, they had finished the task that had begun more than two weeks earlier when don Francisco had carefully tied the feathers together and carried them to the Chapel of the Little Virgin. The feathers had been placed in the chapel for several days in order that this intimate contact with Her would invest them with the necessary power. Now, having performed their task by taking on the evil of these men, they disappeared into thin, gray smoke floating skyward into the day.

As the small boy watched the fire with fascination, don Francisco returned his attention to the bag that hung from his shoulder, picking through it and mumbling to himself. Finally, he pulled a small object wrapped in brown paper from the bag. He slowly unwrapped the package, revealing a small round mirror with an engraving of the Virgin and the words, "The Virgin of Guadalupe, Queen of Mexico," etched on the back. In the bright sunlight, the mirror sent pulsating light waves into the eyes of the waiting men.

The old man hobbled over to them and, one by one, he moved the mirror in a circular motion before their eyes. The men stood still and stone-faced as they saw their reflections flashed before their eyes like a rapidly rotating kaleidoscope. To each man, don Francisco repeated the same barely audible phrase: "Our Lady, Queen of Mexico, Mother of us all, enter into us and give us strength that we may serve You and that we may reveal You to others."

After he had finished, the old man who had been responsible for the final act of transition looked into and far beyond the faces of each of the men, as if searching for the answer to an as yet unasked question. He looked for some clue that only he was empowered to see. With a sudden arch of his eyebrows, which seemed to move his straw hat back on his head, he signaled to don Emiliano that he and the Virgin had done all they could, or would, do. With that, he shuffled back into the house, past the crowd on the porch, sat down in the same chair that he had occupied most of the night, lit another cigarette, and gazed silently into his past.

The dark figures that he had left outside on the patio were no longer ten ordinary human beings dressed in elaborate costumes. They were *Los Negros*. They now were joined symbolically with the countless others who in centuries past had been so honored with this intimate relationship with the Virgin.

Los Negros burst out in music and dance. Their music, dance, and shouts mingled with the ordinary morning sounds of the village, and the people watching knew that they were home at fiesta time.

Several hundred yards away, Celistino was still alone with his dictionary and dreams of the future. While others were busy celebrating a communal rite born out of tradition, he was immersed in a private ritual that had its source in his increasing distance from that tradition.

He was born an *indio*, a *mexicano*, a Nahuatl-speaking Indian. His first clothing was the white cotton pants and shirt of the *indio campesino*. By the time he was five years of age, he spoke fluent Nahuatl and only a little Spanish, and had added a straw hat and *huaraches* to his wardrobe, so that he looked like a small carbon copy of his father. He soon was working alongside his father in the fields, learning through experience the way that was supposed to be his for life. His father used to say, *"El maiz es mi modo,"* meaning much more than simply, "Corn is my way." He meant that the cultivation of corn was for him, an *indio*, the *only* way and to think of doing something else would have made him someone else. It was easy for Celistino to see his father's way as a natural and inevitable mirror of his own future; he, too, would be a cultivator of corn, like his father, his grandfathers, and his great-grandfathers. With a settled future, there was no reason to dream, for although he looked forward to his life with enthusiasm, his early boyhood thoughts were not truly dreams; they lacked those elements of remoteness and potential inaccessibility that stem from a disenchantment with the present and its future direction.

Celistino started school at around the age of seven. But some days his father would tell him that his help was needed in the fields by his family more than it was needed in the school by his teacher, and Celistino looked forward to those days with pleasure. After all, the teacher had many students, but his father had only one son. Anyway, his father used to say that school was only good for learning enough reading and math so that he could not be cheated by the government or by merchants who were always out to cheat *indios*.

But if the events of his early life had been predictable, it was all to change by the time that he was eight years old. That year the land that his father had sharecropped was sold to a man who wanted to work the land himself. His father talked to the new landowner about work, but the man had many sons to help him. Gone in a matter of days was the land that Celistino's father had labored on for almost fifteen years, the land that long had been central to his existence.

Celistino remembered the betrayal and humiliation his father had felt because no one had had enough respect to consult with or even forewarn him. Here he was, suddenly without land, without his life, without his way, and when he looked at his only son and said, "I am no longer a *campesino*," Celistino knew that his own future was also unsettled. So he started to dream.

Like many other *indios* in the region, Celistino's family moved to Jonotla where there were economic alternatives to corn cultivation. Jonotla was the region's political and economic center, and as such, provided more opportunities for wage labor than did most of the other villages in the area. *Indios* and *mestizos* alike who found themselves caught in the vise of economic uncertainty caused by an increasing population, soil depletion, and an increasing inequitable distribution of land were forced to search for new means of support. Jonotla was frequently the starting point in this search, which for many did not end until they reached the poverty-stricken barrios of Mexico City.

His father took a job working in the fields and coffee groves of a relatively wealthy villager, a middle-aged man for whom one of Celistino's distant relatives had once worked. Because of this connection, and because he was a hard worker, Celistino's father soon became a favorite with his boss. They established a kind of patron-client relationship, which, although inequitable, fulfilled certain needs of both men. The patron had a loyal worker and supporter, and Celistino's father had a secure job and the sort of respect that went along with his association with a man of such high community stature. But at the same time that he received such benefits, his father despised his total dependence upon the goodwill of another man. Outwardly he found security in his new economic relationship, but inwardly he must have felt less than the man he had always thought himself to be.

When Celistino was twelve years old, his father died. But there was a disagreement as to exactly what caused his death. Celistino was certain that *los aires*, the sickness-bearing winter winds had claimed his father. His mother did not agree. Celistino remembered that on the night before his father was buried, his mother had talked incessantly, even when there was no one around. Much of what she said was incomprehensible to the twelve-year-old who was having difficulty grasping the full meaning of his father's death. Much of what she said Celestino had forgotten. But he did recall that as his mother stared at the body of her husband, who had a small cross clasped between his worn and rigid fingers, she repeated the words, "My poor husband, my poor husband, you could not live in this way. . . ."

Eighteen years later, that was all that Celistino could

remember about that night. The rest was but a memory which could not be fully measured by words. He could not or would not explain what his mother had meant, for to Celistino it seemed that in Jonotla they had a better house, more money, and more security than previously.

"Like all women, my mother was too sentimental," he would now say, as if this were a full explanation for her sorrow. "She longed for the old way, but we really had it better here. She was a woman, a mother, very sentimental. She thought . . ." and his voice halted as he groped for a new beginning. "My father's death was simple—it was *los aires* and nothing more. He had been working very hard, and it had been very cold and wet. It is that simple." His voice spoke with authority and confidence, but the thin veneer of words seemed only to comfort and shield him from his true feelings about his father's death and, more immediately, about his own life.

After his father's burial, Celistino quit school and worked full-time in the coffee groves that graced the steep mountains and small valleys that surrounded the village. He recovered quickly from the tragedy and at least outwardly enjoyed his new position of importance in his family. If anything, his father's death had increased the security of the family, as they were virtually adopted by his father's boss. Celistino knew that he would always have work and food as long as the older man, whom he took to calling *el patrón,* was alive. His hard work and his proper attitude of deference soon made him a favorite with the patron, and they spent an increasing amount of time together. The patron treated him more like an adult than his own father had, and this he enjoyed. Celistino remembered it as one of the most pleasant periods in his life. Once again, his future seemed settled.

But just as they had before, the unpredictable events of life shattered his security. *El patrón* was slain in the streets by a drunken, pistol-wielding young man, and Celistino's newly ordered existence was washed into the gutter along with the blood, absorbed by the dirt and animal dung between the cobblestones.

A series of public arguments, verbal duels, had preceded the killing. The younger man was feeling brash and cocky, and attempted to ridicule *el patrón* when they were drinking in the same store. It was a mistake. In a short while, with adept sarcasm and wit, Celistino's employer had reduced the youth to a refuse pit of disgrace. On numerous subsequent occasions, the young man attempted to strike back at his opponent without success. He was repeatedly humiliated in full view of the entire community, and he soon acquired the reputation of a *pendejo*, a man who was incapable of functioning as a man should. He became a mere shell of a man, possessed, manipulated, and exposed by the manliness, or *machismo*, of *el patrón*. Like the insect caught in the spider's web, the more the young man struggled to extricate himself, the more he became entwined in his own deathtrap.

Finally, he had but one means of salvaging his honor. Concealing a pistol beneath his worn sarape, he waited for twilight when his possessor was known to walk to his daughter's house to share an evening of food and conversation. As the sun bade good evening to the village, Celistino and his employer began their last walk together, neither of them suspecting the tragedy that awaited them. As they walked, Celistino graciously laughed at *el patrón*'s recollections. When they turned the corner toward their destination, Celistino saw ahead of them the young man leaning against the white-washed wall of don Niceforo's store. The strong wind and the *refino* he had been drinking all afternoon made his body gently sway back and forth. Already several men had gathered on the opposite side of the street, for they knew he was determined to make this the last encounter with his enemy.

Celistino whispered a warning to his companion, but he got no response. As they continued their slow walk down the cobblestoned street, *el patrón* chatted idly; his eyes ignored his young adversary.

Somehow the news of a confrontation had spread throughout the village. Crowds gathered at both ends of the street, as if filling the grandstands for a major sporting event. Those who gathered, however, were not just spectators; rather they were judge and jury in this final contest. The quality of manliness is judged by others, and thus this jury of peers had formed for this duty. The entire process leading up to this day had been a public spectacle, taking place in the streets, in the pool hall, and in local stores. Now the young man was making certain that his final fight was a community act as well.

When Celistino and his companion approached the young man, he stepped in front of them, forcing them to stop. Celistino feared the worst, and he thought of how stupid the entire game really was. He wanted to cry out and stop time so that he could have the opportunity to convince his employer that life was more important than the game. While these thoughts flashed from Celistino's head to his stomach, making him queasy, *el patrón* looked coldly at his adversary and asked patronizingly why the young man dared to stand in his way. It was a senseless question, for everyone knew that he was there to reclaim no small part of himself, his honor, from its possessor. No doubt the laughter and derisive comments of the patron were ringing in the young man's ears, as were his own stuttering attempts to respond to them. Once more the jury had convened, and he would soon extricate his manhood from the trap in which it was imprisoned. He was fully aware that bullets do not stutter, and they leave little room for reply.

It was a senseless question, but it was a part of the script. Neither the young man nor *el patrón* had been left with any other recourse. The young man's manhood had been slowly sucked from him, until only violence would restore some dignity to his name. The patron had been judged the *macho*, and he would retain that judgment even in death, for he would face his doom defiantly and indifferently. The ultimate measure of one's honor is to face the most impossible adversity with defiant fortitude. This is admired even more than the most brilliant triumph. Thus the patron read the lines as they had been written for centuries.

Once again Celistino silently cried out for a respite so that his patron could be convinced to change the script, and improvise in hopes that somehow by writing a new line the inevitable ending of the story could be changed. But the young man was already replying as expected, although Celistino could not or would not remember what he said. Then the young man pulled the pistol from his sarape and with several quick shots regained a portion of his manhood and honor. What was reclaimed by the young man was not lost by el patrón, for he had even increased his honor by seeming to be an unconcerned spectator of his own death. The shots that extricated the young man from his possessor and sent the patron to a glorious victory in death, once again shattered the complacency in Celistino's heart. The crying, praying, offerings, condolences, bitterness, sorrow, and deathly pride that were a part of the mourning period seemed to encircle Celistino without shaking his own emotions. He performed the formalities that were expected of him, but at the same time he felt a strange sort of separation from his own actions as well as from those of the other mourners. An emptiness pervaded his world as thoughts and feelings raced through his body, refusing to slow sufficiently so that he might examine them, understand them, or even express them.

On the morning of his patron's funeral, he sat alone with a spiral notebook and started to chart his future. He wrote and planned and dreamed. The patron's daughter sold the major portion of the family's land and moved to a larger town where she and her family could escape their memories. Celistino thought about doing the same, but his memories lived too vividly in his mind, and he decided that a change in physical surroundings would never really dislodge them. And so he remained.

Gradually he turned further and further away from his past. His father's loss of land, his father's death, and finally the death of the patron had shaken him from the traditional nexus of his *indio* past and cast him unanchored into the depths of a new world. Celistino felt himself to be on the sidelines of life. He had broken—partly through choice, but choice fashioned by tragic circumstance—with his *indio* past, and yet he remained marginal to the *mestizo* male's world. In the years since his patron's death, he had been unable honestly to develop the bravado, the sense of spectacle, the aggressiveness, the combat approach to life that characterize the successful *mestizo* male personality. Somehow the memories that remained deep within the mazeways of his mind continued to beckon him. Though he frequently tried to emulate the *mestizo* male, as when he and a close friend would go out drinking with one another, he always felt uncomfortable in these attempts.

Most of Celistino's dreams on this fiesta day could be summarized in a single word—*commercio*. The dream of being a small businessman and store owner drew Celistino to it like a magnet. It encapsulated all his diverse desires for money, prestige, honor, and sense of worth.

He continued to fill the same brown spiral notebook that he had started on the day of *el patrón's* funeral almost ten years earlier. The plans that were there were only rarely realized. "I am only thirty years old," he wrote, "and already I am tired of working in someone else's mud. Soon I will own a store and land, and then I will have men working in my mud! You will see!" The visions shaped by his words made him smile contentedly, and he seemed outwardly unconcerned that so few of his plans ever became reality. It was almost as if the realization of his dreams was secondary to the importance of the ritual of recording them. The words in his notebook seemed temporarily to heal the painful memories of a broken past and calm the anxious fear of an unsettled future.

Although he frequently appeared ill at ease when he was with others, he was always comfortable when alone with his dreams, as on this December morning. Suddenly, his daughter, Avencia, burst into the room and shouted that *Los Negros* were on their way. Pulled away from his reveries, Celistino could hear the music and shouts of the fiesta.

"Let's go see them," he said quietly, closing the dictionary on his notebook. He took his daughter's hand and they strolled out of the dim room into the sun-drenched street. They hurried alongside other villagers to the corner and waited, straining their necks to see signs of the celebration. Avencia's squeals of excitement made Celistino laugh, and he teased her for being so easily aroused.

Down the street which leads out past *la tierra del campo santo* westward until it turns into a small trail snaking down the mountain toward the Sempoala River marched *Los Negros.* They were headed toward the plaza, shouting, singing, and dancing to the whining fiddle and flute. One among them carried a maypole with crepe paper streamers flying in the gentle morning breeze. The exhausting night of dancing, speeches, drinking, music, food, and very little sleep had not dampened their enthusiasm, for this was the moment for which they had long prepared. The gaiety on their laughing faces and in their rhythmic bodily movements was contagious.

They were headed for the plaza to do the only thing that men who are filled with the fiesta can do—burst out in song and dance. Already the fiesta could no longer be contained as it swelled in their bodies and was expelled in soaring shouts and in pounding dance steps. The spellbinding click-click of the dancers' castanets, the seesawing guitar and fiddle, the haunting wind song of the flute, the pounding of the boots against the smooth cobblestones, and the piercing shouts of *Los Negros* bounced from the mountainsides to the plaster houses and were heard in the souls of the crowd, who could no longer remain just spectators in the midst of a scene saturated with such powerfully traditional emotion.

As the dancers passed the corner on which Celistino stood clinging to his daughter's hand, the squealing crowd joined the dancers in their determined march to the plaza. Their movement down the narrow street was as forceful as a flash flood moving down a dry canyon, and people standing on both sides of the street were swept toward the plaza on the crest of emotion.

The plaza, which on other days had a kind of decaying appearance, was today transformed. The crumbling sidewalks and cement benches, the patchy brown grass, the dying trees, and the fungus-covered circular well went unnoticed. With the fiesta, such things did not matter; for the decay and ugliness was erased by the beauty and joy of the fiesta itself. Even the statue of Benito Juárez, marred by a broken nose and a greenish corroded exterior, seemed to emit a new vitality, as it stood looking out from the north end of the plaza. The inscription, "Respect for the Rights of Others Is Peace," was quite unnecessary today, for at fiesta time peace and consensus seem to reign. The fiesta is communal, and all participants share an identical destiny in the transitory but important triumph that is symbolized by *Los Negros*.

The dancers entered the plaza from the south and turned eastward toward the marketplace. Their symbolic continuity with the past had succeeded in stopping time, for the scene was as it had been for centuries at fiesta time. With one exception: Standing silently next to the marketplace were three large machines—*las máquinas*, as the villagers called them—which were part of the carnival that had arrived a week earlier and would remain for most of this month of fiestas. A Ferris wheel, a merry-go-round, and *las sillas voladoras*, a machine that swung eight chairs and their occupants rapidly through the air, were for the moment motionless. Riding and watching *las sillas* was an

Villagers watching las máquinas

experience that had especially thrilled, frightened, and astounded the villagers, most of whom had never before seen such a contraption.

The carnival was a part of the outside world that had continued to encroach on the village since the completion of the little dirt road the previous summer. Prior to ₁that time, Jonotla had always been separated from the nearest road by a series of mountains that took nearly three hours to traverse on foot. But with the completion of the road, the village found itself inextricably bound to the world outside. At first, the intrusion of that world had been just a small trickle in the form of an occasional car, bus, or truck, bearing such colorful names as "Indian Love" and "Midnight Virgin." However, by December, the month of fiestas, it seemed that the road had finally been discovered as the trickle was transformed into a roaring stream. No stranger to

Jonotla were taxicabs, trucks, all forms of commercial activity, tourists, exhaust-spewing buses, old John Wayne movies, religious pilgrims, itinerant peddlers of plastic wares, silver-tongued politicians, an ice-cream vendor or two, and even *las máquinas*. In short, the modern world had ascended in full fury to the ancient green mountain of Tlaloctepetl.

For now, the carnival rides stood quiet. The colorful animals on the merry-go-round were motionless and the decorated chairs of *las sillas voladoras* remained stationary in the gentle breeze. The fiesta had turned the village inward; the roaring invasion was temporarily dammed. It was the fiesta. *Los Negros* swung naturally into their twisting, winding, bending, stomping dance around the maypole near the silent machines. The crowd grew in size and intensity. The music, the dancing, the shouts, seemed to mock *las máquinas:* "We—*Los Negros*—have known centuries of fiestas! How many have you known?" The shouts of men were carried high above the sleeping Ferris wheel; the women sang secret songs to one another; and children squealed and jumped through the air in vivid imitation of the dancers.

One man who had spent the early morning hours drinking *refino* threaded his way through the crowd past the dancers to shakily but triumphantly grasp the maypole and shout inaudibly to the dancers. Yesterday, he carried heavy sacks of coffee beans across town for twenty *centavos* a load. He ate stale tortillas and shivered the night away in his airy wooden house. But today . . . today his grasp on the maypole held the world together; his shouts gave direction to life itself.

Two men with freshly bandaged heads and hands—no doubt, the result of slightly too much *refino* and bravado the preceding night—held a dirty white handkerchief between them and danced as one.

Celistino remained at the back of the crowd. His interest, like that of the others, was now focused on *Los Negros*. He gazed at them, measuring every step and movement against some remote standard in his mind. His daughter moved into the crowd where she watched with the particular combination of thrill and fright that makes for a child's fascination with the mysterious.

Los Negros had formed into rows of three with the lead dancer alone in front. The straight lines moved forward and backward, left and right, in a complicated pattern of stomping foot movements. Their upper torsos remained as rigid as the silent machines, while their legs and feet pounded out traditional rhythmic stories on the ancient plaza. Their eyes appeared glazed, as if fixed upon some distant morning star. They seemed unaware of their surroundings. They had been captivated by the eternal symbol that they had become. Perfectly and completely, they were *Los Negros*, and the crowd knew them well. Participating with them in the symbolic transformation of time and space momentarily blotted out all other experience. Surely everything that anyone could have asked for was here with *Los Negros* and the fiesta. Indeed, was there anything else in the world?

Suddenly it happened. At first it was the slow, hesitant popping of the generator as it gradually took hold and sent its power screaming into the insides of *las sillas voladoras*. Then came the fearful, delighted shouts of several children who were sent flying through the mountain air strapped to the rusting metal chairs. In only a few seconds the screaming drone of the engine interrupted the fiesta music. No other sound, no other voice, no other song, but that of the machine could be heard in this ancient plaza where men had always lived in the company of sounds now silenced. Those villagers who had only moments before attentively measured the world of centuries past turned toward the loud, methodical sound. One by one, the other machines added their voices to the shattering wail of *las sillas*. Horses and burros tied in the plaza bobbed their heads wildly and pranced with sudden fear as they pulled furiously on the ropes with which they were tethered.

Although *Los Negros* continued to dance, the journey was over for them and those who would have followed. They had abruptly returned, alone and unwelcomed, from their travels into mystical time. They were now only costumed men, strangers in a world that once had been theirs. The weight of centuries could not help them now.

Avencia came running through the crowd and grabbed her father's hand and pulled him closer to the machines. Celistino, nodding his head and laughing, followed her. At the front of the crowd, he stood silently, arms folded across his chest, staring at *las sillas*. It wasn't a clavichord or a Gothic cathedral, but that really didn't seem to matter. It was new, and his face revealed a kind of satisfaction with that fact alone. Then, for a moment, he glanced over his shoulder and saw *Los Negros,* and it seemed as if he had remembered something. Turning once again, he picked up Avencia and moved yet a few feet closer to the carnival rides until the sounds of *Los Negros* and of his past were swallowed by the sounds of the world to come.

3-The Day of the Dead

*The Day of the Dead . . . a mirror flashing
reflections of the hopes, memories, fears,
loves, and vanities of the Living . . . a
candle illuminating darkness . . . a wall
obscuring sunlight . . . a diary of important
moments . . . a celebration of the death
and life that each of us has chosen for
himself. So tell me how you live, and I
will tell you how you will die; tell me how
you die, and I will tell you who you are.*

If the world founded by Ixoceolotl was caught somewhat off guard by the intrusion of technology in the form of carnival machines on that December day, it should not have been. For the inevitable movement of time had already brought to Jonotla many harbingers of the twentieth century, supplanting traditional behavior, ideas, and objects with those of an alien modern world.

For centuries children had carried water from the village wells to their homes in graceful narrow-necked pottery created by local artisans; now they labored clumsily with pastel-colored plastic buckets that did not safely hold the water within them. Inevitably, much was spilled before the youngesters reached their doorsteps. Women whose bare feet had traversed the cobblestoned village streets, unfeeling of the rough stones and the icy winter rain exchanged their hardened calluses for blue and pink plastic sandals. Sarapes, hand woven in geometric designs in the nearby village of

Buyers wearing sarapes at the market

Xalacapan, lost favor to red, green, and blue plaid styles manufactured in San Luis Potosí, a sizable city located far to the northwest of the village, separated not only by hundreds of miles of terrain, but also by years of experience with the modern world.

Young villagers no longer looked forward to a life spent in the mountainous fields that had been the only homes their ancestors had ever known. They began to join the uprooted, unskilled migrant laborers in the streets and factories of Mexico City. Their parents, for so long content with their self-sufficiency, were also stumbling blindly into a broader marketplace of commercial profit. The world was no longer a place with which they could attain some sort of harmonious relationship, but rather it was an obstacle course to be run in the struggle for control and power. They should not have been surprised.

Certainly Celistino had not been outwardly startled by the power of the machines to capture the attention of the villagers. He not only was surrounded by the myriad external changes that were flooding the village, but internally he also was engaged with the forces of change that tore at his soul. He was caught like a twig in a watery whirlpool, moving in circles, now upstream, now downstream, ultimately destined to flow with the powerful current of the future. He no longer wore the clothing of the *indio*; he rarely spoke his primary language, Nahuatl; his dreams were of tomorrow rather than yesterday. For him, what the machines had accomplished was only the inevitable.

Yet there was something deep within that would not quite release him, and so his life hesitated, stuttering on the brink of a new world. Often the struggle between old and new that brought hesitation to his life was fought deep within his mind, as it had been on the Day of the Virgin of Guadalupé. On other days, he was drawn out by certain people and circumstances to engage in the battle openly. Such a day had occurred more than a month before the coming of the machines on November 1, *el día de Todos los Santos*, All

Saints' Day. This day has for centuries been a day of traditional importance during which the bond between the living and the dead is renewed and strengthened. And this year on that day Celistino found himself with people and in a situation that temporarily removed his struggle from the pages of his dream book and out into the world.

One person who represented the past to Celistino and who on All Saints' Day breathed life into his internal struggle was a man named Chalo Garcia Lazaro. Don Chalo was an *indio* who had lived the entire sixty-nine years of his life in Jonotla, never venturing farther than twenty miles north or south to the nearby market towns of Zacapoaxtla and Cuetzalan. For the last fifteen years or so, he had not even left the green-shrouded mountain of Tlaloctepetl upon which the village perched. It was at that time that his deteriorating vision, which for several years had been slowly and increasingly filtering the outside world from his mind, closed and locked the doors of his eyes forever. He maintained that, although the world had become increasingly blurred over an extended period of time, the final loss of sight had been instant.

He remembered how he had awakened one morning to find that his sight seemed to have improved. "Everything was still blurred, but somehow I could see things better than I had been able to for several years. I remember getting out of bed and walking back to where my wife was already making tortillas and coffee. She appeared to me as clearly as the first time that I ever saw her. Everything around her was still fuzzy, but she was clear, as if floating in the foreground of a distant scene. I tried to look at other things, but she seemed always to move directly before my eyes. She had not noticed my presence, although I was standing just to one side of her. It seemed as if I watched her every movement. Neither one of us spoke as we would have ordinarily. Then her face turned toward me as if she had suddenly realized that I was standing there, except that she moved so distinctly and slowly that it seemed very much like a dream. When her face looked into mine, my eyes suddenly and completely left me. She was always very important to me, and I am glad that if God had good reason for taking my eyes, He took them at a time when she stood in such a way before me."

Since that early morning he remembered so well, don Chalo's world had been restricted to the portion of the cobblestoned path between his small, one-room wooden house and the chapel of the Little Virgin at the base of the sacred rock, Tlaloctepetl, some one hundred yards away. His blindness had ended his years of cultivating corn and beans, and he was now supported by peddling religious items and by gifts of food from a few neighbors and relatives. Every morning, not long after sunrise, he carried a small burlap sack to the steps leading up to the chapel. There he spread the contents of the bag—candles, images of various saints, Christ, and the Virgin, and curative leaves and herbs —on the steps to await worshipers at the chapel. On some days, only a few people came, and don Chalo did not sell a single item. Even then, he enjoyed talking to those who did come, as well as to passersby who were on their way to places that would remain always inaccessible to him. But this did not seem to disturb him, for he and the Little Virgin shared a companionship that, he was sure, not even death would destroy.

Don Chalo's wife had died three years before, and since that time, people said that he had withdrawn even further into his sightless world. His blindness, followed by the loss of his wife, whose vivid descriptions used to resurrect his sense of sight, had separated him visually from the external world and at the same time granted him internal vision. People said that don Chalo saw further than any sighted man could or dared to try. They felt that although one world had been shut off from him, another had somehow been opened—a world of the extraordinary, the supernatural, the mystical. Don Chalo actually did nothing to reinforce this view that many held of him, but there were numerous times in which he was strangely inaccessible to those around him, as if journeying far from the situation that was immediately at hand.

Yet don Chalo had not totally cut himself off from the world outside. There were times when his heart opened up and touched those near him. The small, ordinary sounds of life to which the sighted were deafened—the gentle songs of birds, the whistling wind, the crickets, the rain, or even the silence of the warm sun—made him smile and talk in appreciation of the presence of such wonders. It was then that he would speak endlessly and affectionately of the goodness of life in this world.

"There is good life here in the mountains," he was fond of saying. "There is good corn here. Our Little Mother, Our Little Virgin, watches over us and our fields from Her tower in the sky, and in turn we give thanks to Her. Corn is the good life. It was the original gift of God to man, just as the wild berries were gifts to the birds, and the rain was a gift to the wild berries. Every living thing has such a gift, and this gift is all that is needed for a good life. Nothing else is necessary; everything else will follow." Wistful smiles would fold gently across his face as such memories spilled from his mind. Often his thoughts did not make sense to listeners, for the words that they produced were unable to keep pace with the roaring stream of memories. Even at such times, listeners were drawn closely to him, and he to them.

The Day of the Dead had always been an important part of don Chalo's life, and he could not imagine how he could continue to live without the feelings of union with the dead that overflowed his spirit during this fiesta. He had learned long ago that one can never really forget the death of loved ones and that the pain and stinging solitude of separation are tolerable if a day is dedicated to them alone. The day was a celebration of past as well as future, of those times when he shared his life with those who no longer lived, and of that time yet to come when he would be reunited with them for eternity. In this way the inevitable

Don Chalo

pain of death was soothed, if only momentarily, as don
Chalo joined with the dead by reliving his memories, however fleeting, and by projecting himself into his future, however mysterious and frightening. And as soon as this day
ended, he would begin looking forward to the next reunion,
enabling death to provide his life with meaning.

Actually, the Day of the Dead lasted two days. The first
was the day of *los chicos*, when those who died as children,

spared the pain of life, came to visit the living. Although this day was a time of extreme emotion for those who had been separated from loved ones they had barely begun to know, for don Chalo it was relatively unimportant. His wife had aborted a fetus a few years after they were married, but after that they never came close to having children. Don Chalo was certain that the soul of the unborn child, which had come still and bloody into the world, continued to exist in the heavens, and would certainly visit on this first day. But it would come more out of curiosity for a life that it never knew, rather than to strengthen ties with the living. Others who might come on the day of *los chicos*, including an older brother who died before don Chalo was born, were all unknown to him. But one could never be certain of whom might visit—friends, relatives, and perhaps, even an enemy or two. Maybe they would not even bother to come, and if they did, they would certainly understand why he reserved most of his effort and emotion for the following day, the day of *los grandes*, the adult dead.

The initial day passed uneventfully for don Chalo, and that evening he waited anxiously for the morrow. He sat alone with a single cigarette and his memories, when he heard a familiar voice outside his door.

"Don Chalo, are you there? May I come in? Are you sleeping?" Celistino's voice shot the questions out in rapid staccato to hide his nervousness about intruding on the old man. Perhaps, he worried, don Chalo would not welcome his visit. But don Chalo immediately invited Celistino into his home.

The two men exchanged greetings and formalities. Celistino frequently stopped to speak with don Chalo either in his house or on the steps of the Chapel of the Little Virgin. He said that it was because the old man was lonely that he was willing to provide brief company, but it seemed unlikely that that was the whole story. It was not only altruism that explained his friendship with don Chalo. Some intangible benefit was returned to Celistino from this relationship. In the old *indio,* Celistino saw a reflection of his past and an image of a future that for better or worse he might have had. And so they talked.

He had for some time confided in the old man about his dreams of the future, both for himself and the village. It was a compulsive ritual. Don Chalo always knew what Celistino's point of view would be, and Celistino knew that don Chalo would always react negatively to his visions. But still Celistino returned. It was almost as if he wanted to hear another voice, a familiar voice that under different circumstances might have been his own.

"Ever since we were small boys," he said to don Chalo, who sat silently in an old chair, "we have looked down from the height of our mountain toward the lowlands to the east, and we have seen the glow of the electric lights of Papantla and Poza Rica." He became momentarily silent, as his mind seemed to envision the blackness of the night and the lights from the twin urban centers some forty miles to the east.

Then he smiled and turned back to don Chalo, his captive audience. But his listener seemed not to react to his words. Celistino was disturbed by this seeming inattentiveness, and he blurted out in a loud voice, "Is that not right?"

Unmoved by Celistino's momentary irritation, don Chalo halfheartedly reassured him. "That is certain," he said.

Emphatically nodding in satisfied agreement, Celistino continued. "But I can see a day when the whole thing will be reversed. The people of Papantla and Poza Rica will one evening look up into the sky and see a strange light above them. They will wonder whether or not it is a new star, or the moon, or a comet, or perhaps even a miracle. They may be frightened or simply fascinated, but either way they will take serious note of that new, brilliant light throbbing above them as if from the heavens. But, do you know what, don Chalo?" and he again hesitated for a verbal reinforcement from his companion. This time it did not come, for don Chalo's concerns were hopelessly distant. In fear that his words would lose pace with his thoughts, Celistino continued without the expected response. By this time he was quite aware that he was primarily addressing himself. It was *his* dream and would remain so whether or not it was validated by another person.

"They will not be gazing at a new star, don Chalo, but at us! Just think of it! They will look at our night light and see the same radiant glow that we now see over them. And you and I will be in the middle of that brightness that to them in Papantla and Poza Rica will appear like a distant shining star. Our light will probably shine so brightly that we will no longer even see Papantla and Poza Rica. In fact, we will probably not even be able to see the stars. Just imagine! Our own light will be more powerful than the moon and all of the stars together!"

He smiled and turned to see what don Chalo thought of this new age when Jonotla would have the benefit of eternal day through the marvel of electricity. But suddenly Celistino flushed and bowed his head, for he remembered that don Chalo was blind and would never be able to see the wonder that he had described. The old man was so remarkable in many ways that Celistino frequently forgot his blindness.

But today it was not just don Chalo's blindness which numbed his reactions. He had neither the energy nor the inclination to contemplate Celistino's future dream world. Don Chalo's dreams were memories, drawn tightly from the depths of his experiences, and today was a day for memories. They both sat silently taking long, deep draws from their cigarettes—Celistino waiting for some reaction and don Chalo gradually returning from his journey into his mind.

"When I was a small boy," don Chalo said, causing Celistino to smile sarcastically because he had heard this beginning so frequently, "I asked my father about the sun, the moon, and the stars. For some reason, during the first few years of my life, I had always taken them for granted, but one day they became of much concern to me."

Celistino became increasingly irritated by what he outwardly perceived as irrelevant reminiscing. For what did all
of this about the sun, moon, and stars have to do with
the future of the village? And hadn't the future been the
topic of their conversation for the past half hour? The sun,
moon, and stars have been here forever, so what is there
new to say about them? But Celistino reminded himself that
the old man was probably lonely, and so he would stay
for a while longer until he found the opportunity to excuse
himself. After all, wasn't that the reason that he so frequently stopped to visit with the old blind man?

"I asked my father what could happen if they all decided
to leave the heavens," don Chalo continued. "Would we
die? Would there be any light? I was afraid. Do you know
what my father said? He said, 'Do not be afraid, for the
sun is God, the moon is Jesus Christ, the stars are the
saints and the souls of the dead, the earth is the Virgin
Mother, and we are their children. They know what is best
for us, and they will take care of us. Have they not always
been here for you to see, and for me to see, and for my
father and his father to see? Do not be afraid.' That is what
he said, more or less, and from that time on, I was at ease
in my life with the sun, moon, and stars. Many days the sun
watched over me and my fields. Often it made the sweat run
like rain over my body, but it was always smiling, and I
knew that it was good, not only for me but for my corn and
all living things. And many nights I stood looking up into
the face of the night, into the moon and the stars. I even
used to bid them good night, and I think that they also
spoke with me."

His voice was pregnant with warmth and fondness. His
old face cracked with a smile as he looked and leaned
toward Celistino and said, "This electricity that you speak
about may be a great wonder. Who knows? I will never see
it, however, but I will always be able to see the lights from
the heavens, even when the strength of your electricity has
blocked them out, for they are deep within here." And he

pointed to his chest, laughing heartily and finishing his cigarette with a rapid series of inhalations, interrupted only by his smiles.

Celistino shook his head in dismay, excused himself with a few verbal formalities, and was rapidly on his way down the path past the Chapel of the Little Virgin and toward the center of the village. He thought with pity of don Chalo, who would never see the great changes that he felt would surely come to Jonotla and create a world of excitement and opportunity. Yet these feelings seemed not so much directed at don Chalo as they were at himself. In a sense, he feigned pity in order to reassure himself that the visions that he had and that don Chalo lacked were, in fact, good and desirable. If he could convince himself to feel pity for someone who could never share his images of the future, then he might succeed in convincing himself of their ultimate value.

Don Chalo was once again alone. A constant wry smile was cemented on his face. People attributed this characteristically impenetrable grimace to the fact that his blindness did not allow him to be fully aware of his facial expressions. But on this particular evening don Chalo knew why he was smiling. It was as if he alone knew that the sun, moon, and stars were offering him the gift of fond memories, and he gave them a small smile in return.

On the day of *los grandes* don Chalo continued the routine that had been his life for years, but with the apprehensive anticipation of the coming of the dead. He had always been secure and comfortable about his relationship with his wife, so he looked forward to her visit with the same certainty and hopeful expectation with which he awaited the warmth of the rising sun after a cold, uncomfortable night. He worried, however, about the visit of other dead with whom he had partially shared life, but of whom his memories were now dim and distant. Would they feel offended and angered by his inability to strengthen these memories of them, memories that seemed to float unconnected to faces or events? Had he remembered them enough in his prayers and private thoughts? Had he spoken favorably of them to the living?

He had arisen early, somehow sensing that the day was overdue. Usually it was simple for him to tell night from day through the combined use of his senses. His skin could sense the warmth of the rising morning sun; his nose could keenly measure the disappearing dampness of the night air; and his ears overflowed with the varied sounds that were the messengers of the day—the footsteps of people and animals traveling past his door, the occasional shout of joy or anger emitted from neighboring houses, the gentle, but persistent chirping of local birds as they sang their welcome to the day. But this morning the village was clothed in a thick, cold, and damp fog. Under such circumstances, it was difficult for him to sense the transition from night to day. The air remained cold and damp, and people lingered quietly in their houses for additional moments, delaying for as long as possible their entrance into the formidable world away from the dim light and reassuring warmth of their household fires. Even the birds remained silent and uncertain of the day's arrival.

He removed the two sarapes covering him and shivered in the cold morning air. His bare feet touched the cold dirt floor recoiling quickly to the relative warmth of his bed. Muttering to himself, he fumbled for his *huaraches.* Once he found them, he tied the long leather thongs securely around his muddy feet, but the rubber soles of the sandals seemed even colder than the floor. Over his head he pulled the deep-blue, geometrically patterned sarape that he had worn almost daily for as long as he could remember. His hat, placed tightly over the thick white pelt of hair on his head, was his final defense against the cold.

He rubbed his hands together vigorously to warm them and walked into the back of the house, which served as a cooking area. With a match and some kindling, he started a fire in the small stone hearth and put a cup of coffee on to warm. The fire was small, but immensely welcome. Squatting before it, he attempted to recover from the cold dampness. "It is because of the dead," he said to himself out loud, referring to the disagreeable weather. He repeated the phrase as if he wanted it to sink into the seams of what surrounded him. He continued to talk to himself. "The dead cloud the village and make it weep. It is a bad sign for someone. Those who forgot that the dead were coming will surely remember it now, but, perhaps, it is too late. It is probably not their anger, but only a reminder of their presence, a reminder to the living from the dead."

While waiting for the coffee to warm, he forced himself away from the fire to stand at the doorway in hopes of sensing some change in the weather, some sign of the day. He pulled his sarape tightly around his body as the cold wind whipped the fog straight through the house. Pushing its way through the dense air, the solitary sound of the distant church bell, with its slow, weeping, metallic toll reached don Chalo. The bell had rung at the same mournful pace all yesterday, and would continue throughout the remainder of today. The sound throbbed and jolted out of the fog as if coming from some strange, inaccessible place. It was almost as if the world of the living ceased at the edge of the fog, and something else began. The world of the dead was, indeed, close at hand that day.

Don Chalo failed to perceive any change, and, sighing, he turned back into the house where the large cracks between the crudely fashioned wood planks of the wall invited indoors the cold and fog. He approached the altar that, with the help of a neighbor's children, he had decorated the preceding morning, and his hand reached out to touch it. He ran his fingers over every inch of the small table that had been transformed into the altar of the dead. He checked to make certain that everything was still in its proper place, and his movements registered his fear that, despite his careful planning, something would be found amiss and the dead, therefore, would not be satisfied.

Gradually, his hands reassured his mind that nothing had been forgotten. The worn and wobbly table was covered with a piece of black material, and strands of black crepe paper were looped from corner to corner. Leaning against the wall at the edge of the table were three small pictures: one of Our Lady of Guadalupe, one of the Virgin weeping over her dead son, and one of Jesus on the Cross. If don Chalo possessed a photograph of his wife, it too would have been prominently displayed. But he only had his memories of her.

On the left side of the altar, a bouquet of gold and violet wild flowers sat next to five burning candles. The flowers had been purchased the day before from a vendor. In advance of every fiesta, in particular the Day of the Dead, vendors collect small bunches of flowers from the small valleys gracefully secured between the rugged mountains. The flowers speak many languages, and they speak especially well to the dead. Don Chalo said that it was because cut flowers live in both worlds. They have been separated from life by the human hand that broke their link with the life-giving earth, and thus they are in the world of the dead. But who could deny that in their beauty, their touch, their scent, they are also very much filled with life?

Two crosses were also propped against the wall behind the altar. One was a smooth polished cross that he had purchased for his wife at considerable expense. The other was not as finished, but it carried more emotional significance and was, certainly, more potent. It was a *naturál*, a cross formed naturally by the growth of the tree of which it had once been a part. Don Chalo had found it in his corn-field many years ago and it remained, aside from his memories, his most valued possession.

His words remembered that distant day. "It was in the spring and the corn was still very small. I was cleaning the weeds near the trees on the edge of the field when I saw it lying there. My heart ran very fast. It was perfectly formed, not like the plain sticks that others find and pretend to be a cross. This was a sign, and that year I had more corn than ever before. Since that time, it has always brought good fortune to me." Such fond memories always brought a smile to his face, and he seemed to forget about the misfortunes of his blindness and his wife's death.

Despite all don Chalo's preparations, the altar was still not completed. It would only be complete when the neighbors brought the tamales, bread, and coffee which would be offered to the dead to eat and drink during their visit. Tamales were traditional fiesta food, and the dead were certain to appreciate them highly. Don Chalo was concerned because they had not yet brought the food, and so he hurriedly poured a cup of coffee and placed it on thc altar in case he had an early visitor. Then he sat down to silently wait.

The early morning silence, both outside his house and within his heart, seemed to magnify an unintended feature of his reception for the dead. Covering the wall behind the altar were several pages of yellowed newspaper. The paper was from the city of Puebla and was dated December 9, 1966, slightly over a month before his wife had died. She had picked up the old newspaper from one of the village storeowners and had tacked it to the wall as decoration for the fiesta of Our Lady of Guadalupe. Reports of the Soviet Union and the United States, of space exploration, of a beauty contest in Mexico City, and of a child *curandero* who performed miracles in eastern Mexico were frozen in time over don Chalo's altar. Hanging from the pages of the newspaper was a calendar from a furniture store in Zacapoaxtla. On it was a picture of a small, blond boy fishing in a lazy stream running through a countryside of gently rolling hills, a typically serene yet somehow terribly foreign scene. The calendar was turned to January, 1967, the month that don Chalo's wife had died. He had no reason to change the calendar date or to remove the newspaper, and so they remained just as they had during his wife's last days with him. Even though don Chalo was unaware of them, they were especially sensitive memorials, forever marking her death, and on this day beckoning her home for a moment that would never be quite long enough.

Outside, the fog continued rhythmically to swirl around the village. Scattered from the cobblestoned road that fronted don Chalo's house right up to his front doorway were scores of yellow flower petals. Yesterday a neighbor's children had casually plucked them from a bouquet of small wild flowers and strewn them on the ground to form a soft golden path for the dead to follow. The flowers would guide the dead, from the eternity of the other world safely to a place they once called home. The petals were wet and spotted with mud, but even through the mist and fog their glow could be perceived. They would fulfill the purpose for which they were intended.

In the village below, young schoolchildren were gay despite the solemn occasion. There, at the three-hundred-year-old bell tower, the youngsters took turns climbing the steep stairs to pull on the rope that rang the bell. For more than a mile from the village, on this day, it was impossible to escape the bell's reminder of death; the tolling was constant, for just as one of the heavy metallic rings would begin to fade, the next would sound. The mountains were full with the sound of death.

Only a short distance from the bell tower, a large, bulky sarape-covered figure moved carefully across the slippery cobblestones to a building that had large padlocks on the three doors that opened out onto the street.

"Damn bells," he muttered as he fumbled to unlock one of the doors. Only moments before don Angel de la Calleja had been sleeping in the comfort of his bed, warmed by a small kerosene-burning heater, the only such heater in the village. But the bells had begun their solemn chant, and although don Angel had attempted to hide beneath his blankets, he soon surrendered to their sounds and the coming day.

His wife had been awake for some time and had already opened the store located in the front room of their house.

The store was not large, but the income realized from the sale of sarapes, cola, beer, candles, rice, canned goods, eggs, straw hats, rope, candy, kerosene, and toilet paper, combined with the money from the pool hall and the land he owned, gave don Angel and his wife a comfortable life. On this morning, he ate lightly in refutation of his rather huge body, spoke briefly with his wife, and then made his way across the street to open the pool hall. There were no customers, yet; it was too early. But soon there would be. A rainy, foggy day was precisely the sort that brought men out to wait in line for a shot at the tables. Even on *el día de Todos los Santos*. If God would not provide them with the proper weather to work their fields, then how could He possibly complain if they spent their day playing pool?

Don Angel had held the grand opening of his pool hall several years before, and it had immediately become the village *mestizo* men's club. Women never entered—not even Angel's wife—nor did *indios*, although *indio* men would at times stop to gaze through the open doors at the new and

The cemetery

strange game being played inside. They stayed out not because of any overt threat from the *mestizo* men, but because they understood that to enter would place them in a situation which was only poorly understood by them, for it was not only the game that was alien, but even more so, it was the world of the *mestizo* male.

On a day such as today, the hall would eventually be filled with players and spectators, old and young, rich and poor, educated and uneducated. Among them would be don Alejandro, one of the village schoolteachers, who learned to play pool in the bars of Puebla; don Martín, a wealthy coffee merchant; Pepe, a young man in constant combat with the feelings of inferiority that were a result of his deformed leg, and Ambroso, a tall, quiet boy in search of his manhood. They would all come, along with many others, not only to play pool, but also to drink, talk, joke, fight, and reaffirm their manhood by displaying their defiance of life.

Don Angel stepped inside, letting the dim morning light and the cold into the large room where four pool tables awaited the players. Lining the walls were several racks filled with cue sticks and balls. Don Angel ran his hand over the smooth green felt that covered one of the tables. Then he walked to the back of the room, sat down heavily in a small chair, and rubbed his eyes and full face with his hands. Behind him on the wall was a business calendar from one of the principal suppliers of *refino* for the area. On the calendar was a picture of a redheaded nude in profile. In the context of a village where all women wore skirts to their ankles and public modesty was a necessity, the picture was strangely incongruous. But then this was the sanctuary of the *mestizo* males, and the seductive posture and eyes of the nude served to reaffirm their image of themselves.

Don Angel was a unique man. As he walked, each step seemed to implant his bulky frame firmly in the earth, and his pendulant jowls would shake with each movement of his head. His eyes, which seemed forever bloodshot, bulged out of their sockets, as if to embrace those at whom he gazed. He was a model of success for some; to others he was an example of life's misfortunes. He was not the wealthiest man in town, although he certainly could be counted among the richest five or ten, but the diversity of his economic interests and the skill with which he operated them epitomized the *mestizo* ideal of mastery over a wide range of economic pursuits. His good fortune with regard to family and kin—he had many relatives, most of whom were reasonably wealthy and prestigious—and his bad fortune—his family had experienced some especially painful deaths, and he and his wife were childless—were often referred to as examples of "the way things are" when it comes to family life. His contact with the world outside Jonotla—he frequently read national magazines and newspapers, and had made several trips to distant places in Mexico, including one to Acapulco—made him an authority on a variety of subjects, and his advice was often sought. For these reasons, many admired him while others found him an arrogant bore, but there were few who had no strong feelings about him at all.

Don Angel also owned a television, which he operated with his own small generator. It had been the first such set in the village (later the local priest acquired one), and he was quick to point this out to any listener. Actually, he talked about it more than he watched it. Due to the relative expense of generating his own electricity, don Angel reserved viewing for certain select occasions. Periodically he would charge customers from three to ten *pesos* to watch a special event, such as a boxing match, a soccer game, or an afternoon movie, which frequently was an old American Western. And already he was advertising the fact that he would allow paying customers to watch the television coverage of the eclipse of the sun that was to occur the following spring. In fact, there had been such strong initial interest in this idea, from the *indio campesino*, who felt that he would be observing a dangerous and deeply religious event, to the local schoolteacher, who wanted to view a relatively rare natural phenomenon, that he was even contemplating renting one of the rooms in the primary school in order to sell more tickets. The eclipse of the sun was but one more moneymaking scheme, one more demonstration of his singular importance, one more chance to demonstrate his control over life.

Don Angel basked in his notoriety and he rarely refused to express an opinion. With equal ease he would expound on Castro, Communism, and John F. Kennedy, whom he was sure the Communist Protestants had assassinated. In the next breath he would talk at length about the beauty of the beaches at Acapulco and the Holiday Inn there. At every available opportunity, he would proudly display post cards and photographs of his trip to Acapulco. One photograph he particularly liked to show to the men in the pool hall pictured don Angel and a petite, bikini-clad young woman, and in the background a large yacht named *The John F. Kennedy*. One couldn't tell which pleased him more—the proximity of the young lady or the view of the yacht. And it really didn't matter. The entire scene was the important thing, for both the yacht and the girl were equally symbolic of don Angel's accomplishments and his *machismo*. A *macho* is a success in the world of business as equally as in the world of sex, and the photo reminded all that don Angel had conquered both worlds.

Don Angel considered himself to be a *blanco*, that is, a man who could trace his ancestry in "pure Spanish blood." He spoke proudly, even arrogantly, of his great-grandfather who, he claimed, came from Spain to Jonotla in the mid-nineteenth century and quickly established himself as a leader in the community. The entire family had been very careful in the selection of spouses, insuring that their blood would not mix with that of the *indios*. At times, men in the de la Calleja family had no choice but to select wives from the other villages and towns, but usually eligible *blancos* could be found within the village. Consequently, the wealthiest families in town, most of whom claimed pure Spanish blood, were all related to one another through a complicated network of marriages, past and present. Don Angel was related to the three wealthiest families in the village and to six out of ten store owners, as well as to several other relatively wealthy *comerciantes*. He was related to three out of the last six *presidentes del municipio*. His position in the village was secure.

Don Angel and his wife, doña Josefina, both in their fifties, were childless and had long ago given up hope of having a child. Being childless was an economic burden for most, since children are needed to help work in the fields, stores, or other family enterprises. But, more important, it was a social and personal liability, as a man and woman were not considered fully married, and thus fully adult, until they had a child. For these reasons, don Angel and his wife had reared one of doña Josefina's nieces since infancy. Her brother, who had four children of his own, offered them a boy, knowing that a male could carry on don Angel's family name. But don Angel vigorously protested what he considered to be an "artificial" son. So they accepted a female instead. The girl was now seventeen years old, and she continued to live with and work for her aunt and uncle, patiently waiting for marriage. She knew who her biological parents were, and she frequently spent evenings with them and her brothers and sisters. But her home was with don Angel and doña Josefina. Of course, for all of them it was not quite like being of the same blood. The respect, formality, cooperation, loyalty, and, perhaps, even love were there, but behind it all was the constant feeling that they were not quite a true family, tempering those rare but important moments of spontaneous family warmth with a slight sense of distance and formality.

Both don Angel and his wife were extremely conscious of their childlessness, but it affected them in quite different ways. Doña Josefina felt as if she had somehow been tricked and betrayed by God, who had denied her the most meaningful part of being a woman. But her pain was internal, and she did not seem to be overly concerned with her social status as a barren woman. On the other hand, don Angel seemed largely concerned with the judgments others made about his situation. For one could hardly be considered a whole man— a *macho*—unless he were sexually potent, so that don Angel made it clear to other men that the problem was with his wife. He bragged that he had had many sexual conquests and had fertilized offspring throughout the entire country. At times he even compared himself to a painting that he once saw in a book, depicting an Aztec god raining life-giving semen down on the countryside. The men accepted don Angel's stories of sexual potency. How could they doubt the man in *that* photograph, the man with *that* calendar in his pool hall, the man who was *that* much of an able business-man, the man who possessed *that* kind of wit, the man who had demonstrated his *machismo* in so many ways? To do so would have been like doubting themselves. Don Angel strug-gled to convince himself of his virility by convincing others, and they listened and believed so that their ideal could be given flesh and bones. In this way, they needed each other.

At the moment, however, don Angel was alone with him-self, alone except for the incessant bell from which there was no escape. The tolling was here to stay, for this was its day to be heard, even in a pool hall. Was nothing sacred on this Day of the Dead?

He had passed only a few silent moments with himself when he heard loud, laughing voices coming his way. Soon three young men entered the pool hall and greeted him, and he silently nodded his head in return. The players walked around the walls, selecting cue sticks with the care of duelists selecting their weapons. They joked and laughed about the impossibility of even the best cue stick improving each other's game, and soon they were diligently practicing their skills at one of the tables.

These three young men, all still under twenty years of age, were usually the first to arrive at the tables. They played with an obsession interrupted only by the necessities of life. They had jobs with the state government, doing manual labor on the construction of the new dirt road which now ran farther north and west past Jonotla. In their jobs they were quite fortunate, as they were at the age when many young people were forced to leave the village to search for work. But the labor on the road would not continue forever, as even a road must end, and they faced the realization that they were spending their last months in the village of their birth and that they then would be forced to take an irreversible step which would place them squarely in a new world from which they would never return.

Gradually more and more men filtered into the small pool hall to watch and occasionally play. Some of the games were friendly and casual, punctuated with lively small talk. Other games, however, were fiercely competitive, warlike, and full of conflict. Players of these games were drawn to the same table, like vultures to the only carcass in the desert.

Such was the case at one of the tables in the back of the room where two of the best pool shooters in the village were playing. The young schoolteacher, Alejandro, who could make the balls perform dances, and don Martín, who compensated for his lack of finesse with an aggressive and daring style of play, had invited Pepe Alvarado, a young and comparatively inexperienced player, to join their game. Pepe knew that his ability was not on a par with theirs, but he was too proud to refuse the offer to play with them. The more seasoned men had invited him because they knew that he would not be a challenging competitor, as they had come to win money, not honor.

"Who is the fourth?" Pepe asked.

"Who knows? Whomever you desire," replied don Martín. His response opened the door for Pepe to select the other player and established the tone of the game. He could choose a friend and keep the game at the level of congenial competition for a little money. Or he could select an adversary and established a contest that was not only played for money, but for the more basic goods of manhood and life. Pepe had been born with one leg shorter than the other and he walked with a severe limp. His behavior frequently compensated for this fateful affront to his manhood, and now he seized the opportunity to determine the nature of the game. He used it as a way to exact a moment of revenge. When his eyes met those of a tall, thin young man leaning against the wall with his hands behind his back, a broad smile raced across his face.

"Ambroso, my good friend, do you want to play with us?" Pepe asked the youth, and it was evident from the tone of his voice and his menacing grimace that this was no casual invitation. For some time, Pepe had been gently taunting Ambroso in public. At first, Ambroso had ignored the taunts, but as this only fanned the flame of Pepe's irritation, he had finally found it necessary to try to respond in kind. Although there were three other games being played and perhaps as many as twenty men were ostensibly watching them, everyone in the hall was quite aware of the situation between Pepe and Ambroso. They were the real center of attention.

As if it were trying to compete with the growing tension in the pool hall, the tolling bell suddenly increased in volume as it called the dead back home. Ambroso maintained an edgy silence. Pepe, his body tilting in the direction of his shortened right leg, continued, "Of course, if you have something else to do . . . ," and he left the sentence hanging. Pepe's challenge had now been made public, and Ambroso could not refuse to play, for if he withdrew from the encounter it would be more humiliating than anything else that might happen. They stared unflinchingly at one another, both aware of their irreversible positions. For the *macho* lives only as long as the *pendejo* wills it. Silently Ambroso walked toward the table and selected a cue stick from the rack on the wall. Pepe's smiling eyes followed his movement, as Alejandro and don Martín proceeded to rack the balls, their faces revealing the anticipation of the encounter to come. Don Martín removed a large roll of bills from his pocket, selected a single *peso*, rolled it into a tight ball, and tucked it into one corner of the table. Each of the men followed suit, so that all four corners of the table securely held a single *peso* bill awaiting the claim of the victor.

From the first breaking of the balls, it was evident that the thin, fragile-looking schoolteacher, Alejandro, was the master of the table. He was able to sink the balls at will with a truly magical skill. The balls danced about the table as he directed their movements with shouts, curses, and vivid body language. It seemed that the only time he misplayed a shot was when he experimented with something new or when he simply tired of his winning ways. Don Martín would also manage to win a few games on this morning of the Day of the Dead. But it didn't really matter who claimed the prize money. Alejandro was undisputed champion of the pool hall, and don Martín had proven himself for years in countless ways. Neither risked anything but a few *pesos*. The only real struggle was between Pepe and Ambroso.

In a way, it seemed inevitable that the two of them were moving so forcefully toward confrontation. Ambroso was, in many ways, very much like Celistino. His parents clung to the stability of the past, in their dress and use of the Totonac language at home. They congratulated themselves that they had done their best to rear their only son to appreciate what they called the good life—modesty, inconspicuousness, adjustment, self-sufficiency, and respect for the saints and the Virgin. But somehow the seemingly uncontrollable forces that combine to make life had pushed and prodded Ambroso in a different direction. He had enjoyed classes so much that he had actually finished all six grades in the primary school, despite his parents' anxiety concerning such a large dose of formal education. His parents saw only the need for basic reading and math skills, and educational embellishment beyond that was considered not only irrelevant but quite dangerous.

"The teachers come from faraway places, and they fill the minds of our children with tales of bad things," Ambroso's father used to lecture him. "They tell them of the wonders of Mexico City, thinking that they are opening their eyes to the world, when in fact they are blinding them to their own people and *pueblo*. Jonotla is a very sad town because our children are leaving."

Ambroso had become "overeducated" for the type of life that his parents had always cherished, and, although his family never discussed it, his eventual physical departure from the village was inevitable. He could no longer tolerate working in the fields, and his nonagricultural aspirations could only be sporadically fulfilled if he remained. When most young men were starting their families and working in their fields, Ambroso was being jostled from one short-term job to another. In the last year, his eighteenth, he had been a field laborer, a carpenter's helper, a road-construction worker, and a laborer for a commercial truck driver who made runs between Jonotla and Zacapoaxtla. His erratic employment was a consequence of both the economic situation in the village and his restlessness. At present he was unemployed, and so he spent most of his time attempting to prepare himself for the full entrance into his new world. He imitated the *mestizo*, at times quite awkwardly, as when he wore calf-high rubber boots, tucking his pants legs neatly into them, and walked about town with an overly measured defiance and pride. Unlike Celistino, he outwardly appeared more comfortable in the new role that he was so actively pursuing. No doubt he would eventually succeed in extricating himself from his past, becoming submerged beneath the waves of rural poor instantaneously transformed into urban poor in the barrios of Mexico City.

For the moment, however, his future was not in Mexico City; it was here directly in front of him, in the village of his birth. Pepe was an obstacle to Ambroso's future, for Pepe *was* what Ambroso, in part, hoped to become. Pepe had willingly exposed his manhood to Ambroso, and it waved, like the cape of the bullfighter, in the breeze of the pageantry of life and death. Ambroso overwhelmingly lost the first game, and although Alejandro took possession of the four *pesos*, Pepe had begun to claim possession of Ambroso.

Pepe remained silent throughout the first game, managing only a sly smile and a slight lifting of the shoulders whenever Ambroso made a poor shot. Ambroso had feebly attempted to counteract his poor play by gently ridiculing himself. Perhaps, in this way, he could partially diffuse the attack that was sure to come. But as Ambroso began the second game with a particularly inept shot, Pepe saw the opening and seized upon the moment.

"Son of a burro, Ambrosito," Pepe frowned in mock disappointment. His addition of a diminutive to Ambroso's name was, under the circumstances, an obvious assault.

"You are not playing up to your usual mediocrity. The cue stick is not a *machete*, and the balls are not brush to be chopped away. Or can't you *campesinos* see that?" Pepe continued with a sharp cutting edge in his voice. Ambroso avoided eye contact with Pepe as he turned and slowly chalked his cue stick. Receiving no response after allowing for the opportunity, Pepe grunted in derision and leaned over to make his next shot.

Celistino, moments before, had left his house and walked the fifty feet to the pool hall, stopping only to exchange niceties with don Vicente, the pork butcher. Now he stood motionless in the open doorway, his back toward the cold and the sounding of the bells. He had never been confident enough to try his hand at the game, but he frequently came to the hall hoping that his appearance would be accepted and that he himself would be accepted as a *mestizo*, as one of them. He always performed bravely, keeping a small, crooked grin on his face and occasionally attempting sarcastic, verbal barbs at the players who were having a poor game. The men in the hall generally tolerated him, acknowledging his feeble attempts to participate with various verbal and nonverbal signs of agreement. He well understood the superficial nature of their acceptance of him, but it was nothing new or unusual in his life.

One of the young men playing at the front table saw Celistino standing in the doorway, and he gave a small whistle greeting which was immediately returned by Celistino, whose confidence was considerably bolstered by his inclusion in this form of communication. His sly smile became even more exaggerated, and his eyebrows arched subtly.

Seeing don Angel slouched in the chair toward the back of the room, Celistino made his way past the players to where he sat. For a very long time, Celistino had admired don Angel, but it was only within the last year or so that he had garnered sufficient nerve to approach the object of his admiration. Several months ago, Celistino had asked don Angel for advice concerning the operation of a store, and the older merchant, who Celistino imagined to be everything that he himself desired to be, had responded with long, windy gems of business wisdom, obviously enjoying the attention given to him by his young admirer. Since that time, the two of them periodically talked with one another about bookkeeping, land value, thrift, Acapulco, Communism, and the relative advantages and disadvantages of giving credit to customers. Celistino had even begun to think of himself as a virtual equal to don Angel, often disagreeing with the storekeeper's advice. For don Angel, the relationship served primarily to fill the voids in a relatively leisurely day, but for Celistino it served to bolster his meager sense of self in the new world that he had reached.

The two men greeted one another, and after a brief pause, don Angel continued, "Ah, Celistino! You are just the man I wanted to see. Do you remember that the other day we were talking about the Aztecs and their magnificent art and culture? Well, I have something to show you that will make your heart race! We can become very rich men with what I have found!"

Celistino eagerly followed don Angel over to a corner of the room. As he walked behind the hulking figure, he noticed that the eyes of the men in the hall followed him as if they could see something that remained invisible to him. But why should he worry? After all, had not don Angel— the man who had been to Acapulco and who owned a television set—selected *him*, Celistino de la Cruz, from among these many men to whom to reveal and share his discovery? He tried to look as if he felt his importance as he walked past and nodded to Ambroso and Pepe, who had momentarily declared a truce.

Don Angel dug through a pile of old blankets and empty boxes until he finally extracted a long, narrow wooden box from beneath. Written in bold letters across the front of the box was the label, "Aztec Artifact." Celistino gave a questioning glance at don Angel, who reassured him, "Yes, yes, it is authentic. I found it half-buried in the countryside yesterday, and it is an exact replica of a rare and valuable artifact that I once saw in a museum in Mexico City. You and I are going back to look for more, and when we sell what we have, we will both be rich men."

Celistino's face displayed enthusiasm for the visions created by don Angel's words as he was handed the box. "Look for yourself," don Angel prodded. The room was curiously quiet as the players chalked their cue sticks in unison and watched the exchange between the pool-hall owner and Celistino. Celistino excitedly lifted the cover from the box and gently removed the object to hold it to the light. In his hand was a two-foot-long plaster replica of a penis. In a moment, the entire building seemed to tremble with the resounding laughter of the pool players.

Celistino managed a weak laugh at himself, but it was artificial and strained. He looked up into the face of don Angel, with whom he had briefly felt allied, and was pierced by his grinning smile and then rocked by a wave of uproarious laughter. They stood there for what seemed to be a very long time, the large shadow of don Angel bouncing with laughter and the smaller one as quiet and inanimate as the object it held.

Celistino returned the box to don Angel who continued to smile broadly. Turning to the side, he moved quickly to lean against the wall and stare blankly at the men who had by now resumed their own battles. For a brief moment, Celistino had felt welcome; now, once again, he felt like a stranger among friends. He wanted to flee immediately to the comfort and security of his empty room, where no one could penetrate to question the meaningfulness of his dream book. He wanted to escape from the depths of solitude in which he now found himself. It was the most dreadful of all kinds of loneliness, where one is surrounded by friends and acquaintances yet emotionally remote from them. Still, even now he could not yield to his inner desire to flee, and so he remained, silenced and stung by the lingering weight of his past.

Pepe turned once again to try to goad Ambroso into verbal combat. He seemed to have drawn some strength from the humiliation of Celistino, for Ambroso and Celistino were known to be close friends, so that to a degree they shared each other's fate. The incident with Celistino could very well have weakened Ambroso's resistance to Pepe's verbal thrusts, and so he renewed his attack.

"Ambrosito, my son, I am surprised that you are not playing better today," Pepe shouted into Ambroso's face. "You are supposed to be winning today, for it is *your* day—the Day of the Dead!"

"Perhaps you should go home and eat some of your mother's tamales for strength," Pepe continued. The men in the room were beginning to warm to the spectacle which they would later judge; they reinforced the developing battle with small nonverbal gestures and half-hidden laughs. Pepe appeared concerned that Ambroso refused to reply to his verbal jabs, for the exhilaration of combat and victory is removed when one's opponent surrenders peacefully. The men were also concerned, for if Ambroso continued his silence, they would be judging a man who had already pleaded guilty. They had come to the pool hall this day to do what they believed that they did best—act like men—and Ambroso's silence was depriving them of the complete attainment of that end.

"Pepe, you learned to play billiards from your sister," one of the men shouted out, hoping to spur Ambroso into battle by providing him with support. Of course everyone understood that the support was transparent and would be withdrawn as soon as Ambroso entered the battle on his own. He remained silent. Celistino tried to edge unnoticed toward the door.

"Ambrosito, will your sister's dead boyfriend visit your home today?" Pepe spoke in reference to Ambroso's younger sister's fiancé who had died suddenly and unexplicably the year before.

"Yes, I suppose so," Ambroso quietly replied, almost as if he had forgotten the circumstances which he was in.

Pepe grinned broadly. "What did he die from, Ambrosito? You can tell us; we are all friends." Ambroso did not reply; he made several good shots, sinking three balls in a row, but the game, which had served as a springboard for the battle, was now of secondary importance.

Pepe turned away from Ambroso and observed the men leaning against the nearby wall. Don Angel, who dwarfed the small wooden chair in which he sat, dozed quietly, uninterested in that which did not more directly concern him. Celistino avoided looking at the table, but his obvious uneasiness betrayed his feigned lack of interest. Pepe spoke, more to the men than to his opponent, something like a lawyer addressing the jury. "Before he died, your sister's boyfriend told me of his symptoms, and, believe me, they were symptoms very painful for a man." He paused to allow his remark to sink in. One by one, the men smiled and nodded encouragement to Pepe.

"Perhaps, you should ask your sister what he died from, for if anyone knows she will." Pepe smiled as the words seemed to curl from his crooked lips. "Do you know what I mean, Ambrosito?" he pursued his opponent.

The pool hall seemed extraordinarily quiet, amplifying the sound of the tolling bells. Finally, Ambroso broke his painful silence.

"Pepe, in my mother's name, if you continue this talk about my sister, I swear that next year you will come with the other dead to eat tamales and drink coffee from your mother's altar." Ambroso appeared flushed and ready for some erratic move. His response meant that the bull was still alive and willing to fight, but it was hopelessly weak, for it revealed too much of his emotions. It was the response of the wounded bull that loses its calm and becomes reckless.

Celistino, who had stood motionless during this interchange, suddenly excused himself from the pool hall and walked out into the fog-shrouded street. He paused to exchange greetings with several unknown, ghostlike figures that were passing only a few feet from him. He tried not to run as he heard Pepe call Ambroso a *tonto*, a fool, which not only insulted his intellect but also was a denigrating reference to his *indio* parentage. It was a serious thing to say, for now the pattern that would govern the relationship between Pepe and Ambroso was irrevocably established. Celistino pushed his hands beneath the front of his sarape and walked up the hill toward his house. He did not care to see or hear anything further. A roar of cold laughter came from the pool hall; the verdict was in, and there was little doubt who was now condemned. Celistino turned and looked back toward the hall. The dim light from the lanterns inside barely penetrated the swirling fog outside. Now the only sounds coming from inside were the heavy thuds of the balls. Celistino turned back to his course once again, propelled forward by the bell tower's molten sounds of death and the pool-hall sounds of living men.

His fear and anguish were locked tightly inside his body, although he could not prevent some of these inner feelings from showing on his face. Fearing a mass exodus of emotions, he redirected his anger toward the most obvious target. "Stupid bells," he shouted, "why can't they give a man a little peace?"

The sudden rush of speech jolted him into realizing that he was still in the open street. He glanced around, embarrassed that someone might have heard the outburst. Quickly he opened the crude wooden door to his house and slipped quietly inside. He could hear his wife, Eudalia, and his daughter talking and laughing in the cooking area, where they had spent most of the day around the small fire that was the only source of heat.

Silently he moved into the room that had once been the doctor's office and opened one of the shutters to allow a little light to filter in. The fog and mist-shrouded cold entered with the dim light. Celistino did not seem to notice. External things had, for the moment, lost all importance. He opened his brown spiral dream book and started to write:

"There can be no doubt as to what the future of Jonotla will be. In one word—progress. The old men like don Chalo live only in the past, and, God have mercy on them, they will never see the future. But I must be ready. Then I will be carried by the power of good fortune to a position of respect and prominence. Perhaps then, others will listen to me. For now, I must prepare. Plan No. 1. . . ."

And here he remained, alone with his future, for the rest of the Day of the Dead. Despite his concern with the future in an odd way, he was brought closer to don Chalo. His dream book sustained him against the threat of solitude just as the fiesta of the dead did don Chalo. In their own ways, they both refused to embrace the idea that solitude is the basic condition of life, a belief that had so permeated the pool hall. Once again Celistino was temporarily suspended in the whirlpool of the present, and yet it was certain that time would inevitably move him downstream where the barricades against the threat of loneliness would be dissolved and the condition of solitude embraced.

At the upper edge of the village, don Chalo sat in his airy wooden house. He had patiently gone about his chores all day, waiting, reheating the coffee and tamales, and waiting some more. Finally he seemed to be growing impatient. Many dead had already come and gone, but the only one that really counted had not yet returned. Thoughts tumbled through his mind like water in a shallow mountain stream. Was she angry with him? Did he not think of her often enough? Did something happen to her in the Valley of the Dead? He stood hesitantly and ambled over to the altar where the tamales and coffee grew cold in their vigil. Because he was hungry and because tamales were a rare treat, he picked one up, peeled the corn husk wrapping from it, and eagerly ate it. Although his neighbor had prepared them for the dead, he was certain that they would understand, for they, too, had once been alive. To be sure, he had eaten a few of the tamales, and he should have had on the altar several additional candles, as well as some picture of his wife, but the dead fully understood the weaknesses and the difficulties of the living. Surely they, including his wife, would see the goodness of his intentions and, thus, feel sufficiently remembered. They would seek no retribution. But to ease his doubts, he went to the hearth and brought a pot of freshly steamed tamales and placed them on the altar next to the picture of the Weeping Virgin. He opened the lid and the white steam rushed upward, mingling with the swirling fog, and steamed the glass on the front of the picture until the Virgin gradually disappeared from sight.

His manner was almost childlike as he sat waiting. He was completely still with his wrinkled hands crossed gently on his lap. His face combined both the ravage and beauty of a long and difficult life. It was the face of a child, filled with unbounded joy and wonder, and it was the face of the aged, creased with emotion and a sense of closeness with the end. His warm visage seemed to ask of life, "What *is* the answer?" while his child face smiled and replied, "What was the question?"

It was evening before don Chalo sensed a sudden but subtle change in the day that until now remained so constant. It might have been a slight pause in the cold wind that had blown all day, or a small gap in the damp fog that allowed a momentary ray of warm sunlight to touch his house. He was sure of only one thing—his long silent vigil for his wife had finally ended. His head turned toward the open door to greet her, his blind eyes filled with tears. And like the new light of the rising sun spreading over a mountain meadow, unrestrained joy swept over his face. He said nothing, greeting her with silent memories alone.

Below in the village, Celistino sat in the center of the empty room and wrote boldly of the future. Alone with his dreams he was calm and self-assured. The men in the pool hall continued to do battle with one another, prodded on by their conviction that solitude is the very condition of life. Don Chalo sat with his wrinkled face turned toward the open door; the clouds filled the room, the tamales steamed; the rain dripped onto the dirt floor; the bell tolled distantly; and the wind softly nudged the path of flowery gold among the rocks.

4-Looking for Centavos

For what do we look and why?
Questions only echo themselves in reply.
Still we move through the darkness
with our solitary light, like a cold,
deep pain across the ancient hills of
our minds. We move slowly, persistently,
fearfully, alone, life travelers with
such a long way before we are home.

During the winter months, Celistino disappeared into his work in the groves of coffee trees scattered throughout the countryside wherever the land was relatively flat. Only several times had he spoken with his friend Ambroso, and even then only about the weather, work, and coffee beans. He had never once asked him about that day in the pool hall nor about any subsequent encounters with Pepe. Because of what he had heard from others, Celistino knew that things were not going well for Ambroso. He heard that Pepe had continued his assaults and further drained the manhood and honor of his adversary. Ambroso seemed so distant now, and Celistino did nothing to try to bring him closer.

Celistino had also managed to limit his contacts with don Angel to those routine occasions that are necessary in a small community. He still frequently traded at don Angel's store and had talked to him once or twice about work, but the friendly discussions they used to have never occurred again. Their talk was limited to formalities, and although neither man ever mentioned it, that day in the pool hall remained as a barrier between them.

The months from December to March were when the coffee beans ripened, and, thus, there were relatively abundant opportunities for wage labor. It was during this period that anywhere from fifty to ninety percent of a family's cash income might be earned. Although he was short, Celistino was solidly built, and his strength, youth, and willingness to work had provided him with a good reputation, so that he had little difficulty hiring himself out to pick coffee beans.

Even so, from December through February he had worked only forty-two days. Of the remaining forty-eight days, thirty-three had been either too wet, too cold, too foggy, or more usually a combination of all three, to work efficiently. The other days had been spent celebrating various fiestas and visiting relatives in nearby villages. But almost any day that he wanted to work, there had been work available. This was in marked contrast to the summer when he would be fortunate to find even a single week's employment. The prospect of a relatively unemployed summer, however, never seemed to bother him, for he knew that as long as God favored him with good health and youth he would be able to earn the two thousand *pesos* or so that were needed to support his family. Besides, he enjoyed the free time that the summer afforded him to spend with his family, friends, and relatives, as well as time alone with himself. He never seemed outwardly concerned about that day when his face and body would reveal the passing years and the landowner would turn to younger men. But inwardly he knew that without land, his economic future would always be insecure.

On this particular March day there were still ripe coffee beans weighing down the branches of the *criollo de la sierra*, but winter was making one last effort to be remembered, clothing the village in an early morning chill that discouraged Celistino and others from going out into the fields. He spent the morning leisurely at home, tending his sow and her five small piglets. He had purchased the sow the pre-

Children playing—coffee beans drying in the background

vious year as part of one of his elaborate schemes to accumulate enough weath to enable him permanently to stop working in the fields. The sow had given birth to six piglets, and Celistino had had dreams of becoming the "pigman" of Jonotla. But the runt of the litter had lost its struggle for its mother's breast, and although Celistino had made a half-hearted effort to feed it, in the end he had simply watched it grow weaker, until it died. For whatever reasons, Celistino had lost interest in his visions of eventually owning scores of pigs. Now, the remaining five young pigs rooted and snorted around the back patio and in and out of the house. Occasionally they would even venture up the stairs to the second floor and into the family kitchen where Eudalia would chase them with a broom, her shrill laughter indistinguishable from the squeals of the pigs as they tumbled down the stairs in front of her. Celistino would eventually sell the grown pigs for a small profit, but like so many of his dreams, his interest seemed to diminish rapidly once the plan had stepped out of the closet of his mind into the world of action.

It was midmorning, and Celistino had wandered out in front of the house to smoke and talk with anyone unfortunate enough to be out in such chilly weather. He leaned against the front of his house, his hands tucked beneath his red, white, and blue San Luis Potosí plaid sarape, and a cigarette drooping casually from his mouth. The streets were still deserted. A neighbor stuck his head out of a doorway, greeted Celistino, and then withdrew once again to the warmth of his house. Celistino hurried to finish his cigarette, for he had by now realized that he would find no company out on an early morning like this. As he turned to enter his house, he noticed a shadowy figure walking up the hill toward him. There was something unusual about the form which turned Celistino's attention back into the street. The cool wind had suddenly blown a dense cloud cover over the village, further obscuring the approaching person. Soon a man—a total stranger—emerged and stopped directly in front of him.

"Good morning. Are you . . ." and he paused to remove a small slip of paper from his shirt pocket to search for some small clue located on it. "Are you Celistino de la Cruz?" he asked.

"Yes," Celestino nodded.

The stranger stuck out his hand. "My name is José Arriaga," he continued in a stacatto voice. "Do you have a few minutes to talk with me?"

"It will be my pleasure." Celistino turned to show the man into his house.

They entered the bare room that had once been the young doctor's clinic. Once inside, Celistino realized why the figure had seemed so unusual. All in all, the stranger's appearance was quite extraordinary. Standing six feet tall, he was extremely lanky and appeared much taller than he

actually was. His hollow cheeks were connected to one another by a thick, drooping black moustache, and his black
hair was slicked back over his ears until the long ends met
with his shirt collar. His clothes were unlike anything that
any villager had ever worn: a black felt hat, a black but-
ton-up sweater over a dark shirt, black denim pants, and a
pair of pointed Western-styled black boots. Don Angel
usually wore a felt hat, but it was a neutral beige color,
with a rather modest, small brim. The stranger's felt hat,
on the other hand, was a very affirmative black with a large,
flamboyantly curled brim. His high-heeled boots explained
why he had been slipping and sliding on the smooth cobblestones outside.

For a moment, Celistino just stared, his mouth frozen in
a disbelieving droop. Arriaga appeared to be straight out of
the movie *Maria Pistolas*, one of the films that had been
brought to the village the previous month by some enter-
prising outsiders. All that he lacked was a large, pearl-
handled pistol in a holster tied securely around his leg.

"Would you like a cigarette?" Celistino finally asked the
man. His hand was shaking slightly as he offered the pack
of cigarettes to the dark stranger. It was a peace offering to
the man who Celistino almost believed could easily transform him from living flesh into nothing more than a small
notch on a gun handle. The stranger accepted with an upward jerk of his head.

As Celistino struck a match and offered the stranger a
light, his confidence appeared to return from its flight
out the back door. "What can I do for you, Señor Arriaga?" he asked, blowing out a puff of smoke with
each syllable. His self-assurance seemed to startle him.
The stranger did not answer as he browsed quietly around
the room while taking long, carefully planned draws on his
cigarette. The silence once again separated Celistino from
his renewed confidence. Worriedly he began to search his
memory for some mistake, some unpaid debt, some unkind
word, or some broken promise that would account for the

visitation of an avenging stranger. But he quickly abandoned this line of thought as the number of such recollections was overwhelming. "Maybe there is another Celistino de la Cruz somewhere in the area," he tried to reason with himself, "a man who has committed horrible deeds against those who now send the stranger in black for revenge." He was about ready to suggest this as a possibility to Arriaga.

"Perhaps you have heard"—the man in black smiled—"that I am the new *comandante** and that I will be here for three or four months?" Celistino breathed an audible sigh of relief.

"Oh, yes, yes, of course, of course, I knew that," he lied. "Doesn't everyone know that?" He shrugged his shoulders and crooked his head to one side in an attempt to hide his surprise.

"Several of us will be rotating in and out of the area on a regular basis," the stranger continued.

"Oh, that is very good, for we need someone around here to enforce the law. There are some real crazy ones who live out in the countryside toward Tuzamapan," Celistino responded seriously. "One never knows what they will do, or when they will do it." Celistino smiled at how well his small welcoming speech had sounded. "If I can do anything to help, just ask me," he concluded.

"Actually, there is something that you can help me with, and at the same time I can help you," the stranger said. "That is why I am here to see you."

Celistino started to worry again. He hoped that the *comandante* would realize that his offer was simply a gesture of goodwill and not a request to be deputized. In his zeal he had somewhat overexaggerated his statements about the country dwellers, but he still did not desire to get linked up with this mysterious man in black. The last *comandante* had been shot during a fiesta some seven years earlier, and even if the people living out toward Tuzamapan were not really crazy, there was enough around who were.

---

* A government police official

"I would be happy to, but you see, I am a very busy man, a poor man, and I must work all day in the fields for my wife and daughter...." he stuttered. The flood of hastily arranged words tried to beat a fast retreat.

The *comandante* smiled broadly, and his black moustache appeared to lift several inches above his upper lip. He unbuttoned his sweater and reached for a notebook that was held by his belt. Celistino saw the white handle of a revolver sticking out of the waistband of the *comandante's* pants. "At least there are no notches," he thought to himself, "but perhaps *comandantes* keep their score in other ways."

Licking his finger, the *comandante* slowly turned the pages of the small book, finally stopped on about the fifth page. "Señor de la Cruz," he continued without looking up, "according to my records, you owned a store for several months, and you went out of business over a year ago. Is that right?"

Celistino was even more confused. "Yes, more or less," he replied. "I did not actually own the store, and I did not really go out of business. It was a special agreement, and things just did not work out. And if I cheated anyone, I did it harmlessly," he continued, trying to cover himself. "I had never kept books before, and it is possible that I made mistakes in what I charged customers, but they were not intentional. Believe me." He was beginning to wish that he had never made that halfhearted effort at, as he used to say, "removing myself from someone else's mud" by trying to operate a store. It had failed miserably, and now he suspected that he might be in greater trouble than ever before. He waited for the mercy of the judge.

"No, no, Señor de la Cruz, you do not understand," the *comandante* said, a big smile spreading across his face. "As far as I know, you are an honest man. I am not here to find out what mistakes you made, but rather to find out which of your customers made mistakes."

Celistino's expression emitted a barrage of question marks

in the direction of the lean black-clad figure that had all but disappeared into the darkened corner of the room.

"I understand," the *comandante* continued, "that you have a number of people who bought items from you on credit and who never paid you. Is that right?"

Celistino nodded three or four times and then finally whispered, "Yes, that is right."

Arriaga continued in an annoyed businesslike manner. "While I am here, one of my jobs will be to collect bad debts, and I would like you to make a list of all the people who owe money to you, with full names, items purchased, and full amount owed." He cocked his head to one side and looked directly at Celistino, who stood motionless except for his rapidly blinking eyes. Celistino was relieved and yet astounded and worried. He had not thought of these debts for many months. Like the death of the runt pig, he had simply chalked the debts up as another loss and moved on to other things. And now here was the stranger in black, asking questions.

It had been over two years ago that his eternal dream had taken a giant stride toward realization. His daughter's *padrino** and his own *compadre*, don Niceforo, had decided to give up his small corner store so that he could devote more time to the development of his other commercial interests. Celistino had made arrangements with don Niceforo to lease the store and its stock with a sort of flexible option to buy if their respective ventures proved profitable. Being *compadres*, their agreement was not at all formalized. There were no papers to be signed, no formal terms, and no new license to be obtained from the local government.

Don Niceforo and his wife had been natural choices to serve as the *padrinos de baptismo* for Celistino's first and only child, Avencia. They were slightly older than Celistino and his wife, and possessed a more established, higher-ranking reputation as well. But, most importantly, don

---

* Godparent

Niceforo had befriended Celistino many times since the death of his patron. Celistino had never really considered asking anyone else to assume this important, binding relationship with his family, and he had been ecstatic as well as relieved when they accepted.

When don Niceforo and his wife accepted Celistino's invitation, they established a twofold formal relationship with the de la Cruz family: first, between themselves as *padrinos* and Avencia as their *ahijada**; and secondly, between themselves and Celistino and Eudalia as *compadres*. Both sets of relationships were governed by *respeto*, an attitude that maintains a balance between respect and affection, formality and friendship, rights and responsibilities.

Consequently, the arrangement between don Niceforo and Celistino for the corner store involved tacitly understood honor and commitment. There was neither room nor need for the mistrust and suspicion that underlies many male relationships, for theirs was an agreement between *compadres*, a relationship that frequently runs deeper and stronger than that of blood. But despite the good faith between the two men, the store had not worked out well for Celistino, and he was soon back working in the fields.

"Well, I am not sure that it is necessary to collect those debts now," Celistino finally replied. "They are very old and are best forgotten." He wrinkled his forehead and waited for the response.

The *comandante* walked over to Celistino. "No, no. It is better for everyone if they are collected. Bad debts make bad friendships, my friend, and I have seen the violent result too often." He put his hand on Celistino's shoulder. "Just give the list to me and I will take care of everything else," he said reassuringly.

Celistino shrugged his shoulders. "I am not sure that I still have the records," he said. "I am rather careless and often misplace things, and I haven't seen my store records

* Godchild

in a long time." He did not really want to bother with the debts even though they were substantial and had certainly been one of the reasons that the venture had failed. And he could certainly use the cash to buy more pigs. But as part of his past, the scheme had become just one more thing for him to forget, and there would be nothing gained by resurrecting those bad memories. Indeed it would only strengthen them and, more important, place demands upon his fragile relationships. And so he garnered his strength and tried to resist once again.

"As I remember," he continued, "I burned that entire box of junk from the store several months ago. I did not think that I would ever have any need for it again. I am sure that the records of the debts were burned with the other things." He frowned and shook his head in mock disappointment.

The *comandante* laughed softly. He seemed to see right through Celistino's defense. Obviously, this was not the first reluctant customer he had seen, nor was it the first time that he had heard that story. "I am sure that you are a reasonable person," he replied, using the phrase *gente de razón* which carried the double meaning of "reasonable" and "*mestizo*." I am sure that as a good businessman you know that money is money and a debt is a debt, no matter who is involved." He paused to let his words settle in Celistino's mind. "And both you and I know that the law is the law." He drew the last sentence out for emphasis, staring unwaveringly at Celistino.

"Maybe I can find them," Celistino nodded as he tried to avoid eye contact with the figure towering above him.

"You look carefully and I am sure that you will find them," the *comandante* said. "I will return later in the day, and you can give me the list at that time. You will see that it is the best for all—you, me, and the law." With that he was gone as quickly as he had arrived.

Celistino walked over to the several cardboard boxes that were stacked in one corner of the room. The top box contained packages of medicine that the young doctor had left. The second box was filled with yellowed sheets of paper, and he removed a brown spiral notebook from it. He slowly leafed through it, passing jumbles of names and figures, until he got to a page with the neat heading "Credit Sales." Running down the page were columns of names, dates, items purchased, and the value of the items. The list continued for ten pages, and although some of the names had been crossed off and marked "paid," the list was still long. Taking a deep breath, he removed a small stub of a pencil from his pocket and sharpened it with his pocketknife. Just as he tore several clean sheets of paper from the notebook, one of the small pigs came grunting into the room. Celistino waited for it to approach him and then gave it a hard kick in the side. "And to think that at one time I wanted hundreds of those little bastards around here," he muttered as the pig went squealing out of the room.

He started carefully to survey the list. Even though his interest in such matters often seemed erratic, he could actually be quite efficient and organized if he desired. In fact, it was in such relatively small matters as keeping records of debts that he was most efficient. The detail gave him a very comfortable feeling, as did the mere fact of recording something safely within a notebook. Dreams, ideas, and money had a remarkable concreteness when recorded in such a way that he seemed to exercise an unchallengeable control over them.

Outside, the early morning chill had begun to disappear and the streets were becoming more active. Some women and children were carrying small buckets of corn to be ground by doña Maria's gasoline-powered grinder into cornmeal for tortillas, while others went to the well in the plaza for water. Several burros passed by laden with heavy bags of coffee beans, and people stopped in at the stores to purchase things and engage in small talk. The shouts of schoolchildren indicated that it was recess time at the school.

Celistino counted the number of names, being careful not to count more than once the many individuals who had bought on credit numerous times. He also combined under one name the different individuals listed who lived in the same household. Proceeding in this manner, he reduced the original number of seventy-five, or so, names to twenty-nine household debts. The debts ranged from a low of six *pesos* to a high of 217 *pesos*.* In just over eight months he had made almost 1,575† *pesos* worth of credit sales that were yet to be paid. This sum represented about one half of what he earned in an average year. But only about one half of the total owed to him would be cleared as profit, for he still had unpaid bills to meet himself. Yet the money owed him was still a large amount, much more than he had imagined.

Dividing the page into four columns headed "Name," "Date," "Amount," and "Items," he started to make the list for the *comandante*. The first name on the original list was Jorge Corona, who owed seventy-three *pesos* for rope, kerosene, cigarettes, and a lot of beer. Celistino lifted the pencil to make the initial entry. "Jorge's wife is a sister of Eudalia's friend, Esperanza," he suddenly thought to himself. "It's best if I forget this one for the time being. Maybe the next time he needs help in his fields he can pay me a little extra." He went on to the next name: Emiliano Santos, forty-eight *pesos* for eggs, a can of salmon, a tin bucket, and several liters of *refino*. Again, he poised the pencil stub over the still empty columns, only to be stopped by yet another realization. "Emiliano is don Niceforo's uncle," he thought, "and my *compadre* pays me back in many ways for his uncle. I can forget this one, too."

He removed his hat and scratched his head vigorously. The next name was Aurelio Tirado, twenty-six *pesos* for candles, kerosene, and soft drinks. Celistino skipped over

---

* Six *pesos* was then equivalent to $.48; 217 *pesos* equaled $17.36.
† This sum was equal to $126.00.

the name without even lifting the pencil. Aurelio had loaned Celistino a significant portion of the money used to buy the sow, and although Celistino had already paid the loan back with his labor, it was best not to press the issue over such a small amount. The next person on the list was the old widow, doña Isabel Castillo. She owed six *pesos* for five bottles of beer. Celistino went on to the next name. Six *pesos* was such a small amount, and he had promised doña Isabel that he would not tell anyone about her habit of drinking a beer once every three or four weeks. He smiled as he remembered her attempts at secrecy. She used to wait outside the store until there were no other customers, place her order for a single beer with a silent nod of her head, and then pirate the bottle to her house as if she were carrying a small fortune in gold. No purpose would be served by including her name.

And so it went. Friends, relatives, friends of friends, relatives of friends, and friends of relatives were gradually excluded from the list. Even Celistino was connected with too many different people in too many different ways. And his relationships, like those of others, tended to be multi-dimensional, linking him politically, socially, economically, and psychologically to others. To attempt to transform such a complex matrix into a simple economic relationship was a complete impossibility. Celistino was certain that these debts would eventually be repaid in some way—if not in cash, then in mutual assistance and a variety of favors and support when needed.

Of course he could have used the cash. The thought of the 1,575 *pesos* and what he might do with them was attractive as well as disturbing. With considerable effort, he cut the final list of debtors down to twelve households owing a total of only 446 *pesos*, a sum equivalent to the pay for over ten days of hard labor picking coffee beans. Even this was nothing to laugh at. He had accumulated some debts with merchants from Zacapoaxtla who had neither the time nor the inclination to view their relationship with him in any other terms except economic ones. These were pressing debts that would have to be paid, leaving him with very little profit even if the *comandante* was able to collect the 446 *pesos*. So the whole amount of 1,575 *pesos* would certainly be helpful. But it bothered him to think in these terms, as he knew that many of those who owed him money would continue over the years, as they had in the past, to repay him in any number of ways. Yet it was a lot of money. He even thought about taking the money and moving quickly to some unknown village. But that would never work, for the money would never be collected all at once—not even by that strange pistol-carrying *comandante* —and Celistino would have to face the glares, gossip, and isolation that would result.

An interruption of these thoughts came in the form of Avencia and one of the little pigs, both squealing into the room. "Avencia!" he shouted, "be quiet! And get that pig out of here! If you want to act like a little pig, then you can move in with the other ones outside. Do you understand, Avencia?" Celistino almost always called his daughter by her nickname, Vencha, unless he was mad at her. His round face glared at her with a menacing contortion.

"Yes," she answered softly as she went running from the room.

Celistino wiped his hand across his face, and the angry expression was replaced by a worried one. He perused the list one last time. Eudalia peeked through the door and asked, "Is anything wrong?"

"Nothing," he replied. She looked at him for a moment, wiping her hands on her apron, and then turned and left him as he was.

His entry into the world of commerce, as brief and incomplete as it was, had extended his contacts outward to individuals whose interests in him were solely economic. That was fine, for they were relative strangers. But now he was being asked to be equally single-minded about the economic relationships he had with his friends, relatives, and neighbors. And he realized that if he could do this, he would have an amount of money that would go a long way toward removing himself from the fields. He also knew that a much greater single-minded attitude is demanded of a successful *comerciante*. Don Angel had advised him of this during the early weeks of the venture, and the list of debtors before him now served as a reminder.

"Credit!" don Angel had said with disgust. "Never sell on credit unless you know that the person has money," he had admonished Celistino. The word was a near obscenity to don Angel. His eyebrows would arch above his bulging eyes, and his lips would tighten at the mere sound of the word. Celistino had often sought his advice during the months that he had been running the store, and one thing that don Angel loved to preach to him about was credit versus cash sales. Don Angel had always been Celistino's idea of a successful *comerciante*, so it was natural that he had gone to him for advice during the initial stages of his days as a novice store owner.

"Imagine this," don Angel said to Celistino during one such advisory session, "a large picture divided in half by a thick black line." He paused to allow time for the creation of the image in both their minds. "On the left side," he continued, "is a picture of an emaciated, unshaven, disheveled, forlorn man wearing ragged and torn clothes and sitting at an empty desk in a bare room." Again he paused, his hands raised to frame the image that was before his eyes. "Now, on the right side," he said as he shifted his hands slightly to the right, "is a picture of a well-fed, clean, neat, happy man wearing a new suit and sitting at a desk covered with neat stacks of money in a beautifully furnished room." Don Angel lowered his hands, stared directly at Celistino, and asked, "Which man would you rather be?"

"Well, the man on the right, of course," Celistino replied without hesitation.

"Why?" don Angel asked.

"Because he is obviously successful. He has money, plenty

to eat, a lot of nice things, and he is happy. The man on the left has nothing, and he is very sad." Celistino was a good student, and the lesson was an easy one.

"Exactly," don Angel said, highly satisfied with the progress that was being made. "Now, do you know why the man on the left is in that condition and why the man on the right is in his?" he continued, like a scholar gently leading his student down the path to enlightenment.

"No, it is not clear why one is prosperous and the other not," Celistino answered. "But, perhaps, it is because the one is smart, and the other is stupid."

"Well, more or less," don Angel responded, like the teacher who receives a correct response but not the one that is wanted. "But the important question is, What does a stupid man do that a smart one doesn't?"

Celistino stumbled for the answer. "Well, he does stupid things," he said finally.

"Let me give you a little more information about the two men," don Angel continued. "They are both store owners like you and me. They both have stores with the same sort of merchandise that is here in my store," he said, waving his hands back and forth through the air. "Now, what does a stupid store owner do that a smart one always avoids?"

"There are many things. Perhaps, a stupid store owner is mean and unfriendly to people, so that they don't like to buy from his store."

"Well, that is true, but there is something which is even more stupid."

"Perhaps, the one on the left—the stupid one—sells his goods for more money than they are really worth. His store is too expensive, so people choose to buy from the man on the right who has reasonable prices." Celistino was certain that he was finally correct. But he was wrong again.

In a way, don Angel had been disappointed that his student had not yet arrived at the desired answer, but he had also been pleased at the chance to reveal the proper response himself. "Well, all of the things that you have said are true," he began. "A store owner who is stupid and unfriendly is certainly not going to be successful. But there is still one thing that will guarantee failure faster than either stupidity or unfriendliness. No matter how smart or how friendly one might be, if he falls victim to this practice there is no way that he will make it."

By now, it had begun to dawn on Celistino. Don Angel's face had already started to form that characteristic grimace as he came closer to pronouncing *the* word.

"Do you know what the store owner on the left would say if he could speak to us?" don Angel continued.

"No, what?"

"He would say, 'I sold on *credit.*'" Don Angel seemed pleased with himself. "And do you know what the store owner on the right would tell us?"

"No, what?" Celistino asked, even though by now he could have guessed.

"He would say, 'I always sell for cash only.'" And so the lesson had been completed.

Don Angel repeated this theme in various ways over the next few months, and if there had been one bit of advice that Celistino should have remembered, it should have been these strong warnings against credit sales. But as Celistino stood there looking at the original and revised lists of debtors, it was obvious to him that the real meaning of the lesson had escaped him. Of course, there had been other reasons for the failure of the venture, including don Niceforo's desire to have the store returned to him, but the credit sales had become oppressively burdensome for Celistino. In fact, don Niceforo had decided to back out of the arrangement partly because he saw that Celistino was getting himself and the store in deeper and deeper trouble. Being *compadres,* don Niceforo had never revealed his concern to Celistino, but had claimed instead that his own business ventures were not working out and that he needed to return to operating his store full-time. To some degree, Celistino was aware of what was going on, but by accepting don Niceforo's explanation, they could—in their own eyes as well as in those of others—both share more equally in the effort and its failure, and thus maintain the balance and respect required of their friendship.

"Celistino, there is a man here who says that he is a *comandante*," Eudalia's voice suddenly interrupted Celistino's thoughts. She sounded and looked a little puzzled and a little worried. Celistino walked briskly to the front door.

"Come in, come in," he said as he motioned for the *comandante* to pass into the side room.

"I am here a little early," the *comandante* replied as he walked past Celistino, "but I was passing by, and I thought that by now you might have that list ready for me."

Celistino frowned and motioned for his wife to leave them alone. She hesitated and then made her way toward the steps leading to the second floor. Her husband had been behaving strangely that morning, and now he was being visited by a *comandante*. Not knowing what was going on, she was becoming increasingly concerned.

Celistino waited until he could hear the floor creaking above his head from the weight of his wife's footsteps. "Yes, yes, I have the list," he finally began. "But it is not very long, and there is not much money involved, and I was thinking that maybe I could just go out and collect the debts. I know all of these people, and I could do it myself." It was his last attempt at resistance.

"Señor de la Cruz," the *comandante* said, smiling again, "I thought that we had already discussed this." His smile broadened into a condescending smirk. "Friendships sometimes get in the way of these things," he continued. "Now, if you try to collect, you will either be unsuccessful or you will lose some friends. But if I do the collecting, then I am just doing my job and who can blame you for that?"

Celistino could tell that there was no use in resisting any further, and besides the *comandante's* argument did seem to have a certain logic to it. "Very well, here is the list," he said as he handed over the sheet of paper. "But there is no hurry. Take your time," he added. The words did not fully convey the meaning he intended. The thoughts behind the words were really more like, "be careful . . . don't hurt anybody . . . don't anger anyone . . . be polite . . . tell them that I send my greetings . . . don't push it." But he could not say what he felt, for if he did, the *comandante* would only laugh again. So he surrounded his thoughts with what he hoped would be the most acceptable words and trusted that the *comandante* would somehow understand their implicit meaning.

"Don't worry," Arriaga said. "This is my job, and I know how to go about it." He looked over the list for a moment, glanced up, smiled, and stuck his right hand out to Celistino.

As he was accustomed, Celistino extended his hand flatly and limply, but he was met with a firmly cupped hand and a powerful grip. The two contrasting ways of performing this apparently simple and routine ritual seemed to symbolize the dilemma with which Celistino had been struggling that morning and, indeed, his entire life. He smiled to cover the pain.

"I will see you in a day or so to let you know how things are going," the *comandante* said as he left the room. Celistino followed him to the door. "You do understand," he continued as he placed his black hat back on his head and stepped out into the street, "that there is a customary collector's fee of twenty percent. That means that you pay me twenty percent of what I am able to collect. It is a standard practice for this kind of service."

"Oh, of course, I understand," Celistino replied without a sign of surprise. He hadn't known about the collector's fee, of course, but it was the sort of thing that businessmen should know. And so he lied.

He closed the door again, pushing the light back out into the street. The *comandante* had earlier explained why the collection of the debts would be good for the law, and

Celistino could grasp the argument that laws must be enforced since they are for the good and protection of everyone. And now he understood why the collection of debts would be good for the *comandante*. But he still had doubts about whether or not it would be the best for him. He would just have to wait and see.

He returned to the room in which he had already spent most of the day, and stood quietly with his hands stuck into the pockets of his baggy blue pants. He stared at the floor.

"Is anything wrong?" Eudalia interrupted again. "What did the *comandante* want?"

"Oh, nothing important. He just wanted to ask me a few questions about the time I was running don Niceforo's store." He smiled reassuringly. "You know that *comandante* is a strange man. Did you see the way that he was dressed?"

"Yes, yes, like he was going to a funeral!" And they both broke into loud laughter.

They talked for a while about the *comandante*, the pigs, the weather, job possibilities, their daughter's behavior, and a few other family matters. Eudalia glanced out the back door at the clearing sky.

"I think that I will wash some clothes," she said. "Maybe you should go and cut some weeds for the pigs to eat," she suggested. But Celistino had other plans.

"I think that I will go visit don Chalo first," he said as he yawned and stretched his arms overhead.

"Why?" Eudalia asked with a puzzled expression.

"Oh, just to keep the old man company. It's been a long time since I visited him and he gets lonely up there by himself." He picked up his straw hat and tucked his shirt into his pants. As he walked out of the door, he turned to Eudalia and said, "The *comandante* looks like he is going to a funeral! That's good! I wonder who has died?" His laughter followed him out the door and up the street.

He always gave the same reason for visiting don Chalo. It was always the old man who was lonely and in need of companionship. But on such occasions, Celistino was like a river with a calm surface and a strong, turbulent undertow. His external tranquility concealed a deeply troubled heart. He would always say that don Chalo needed him when in reality his need for don Chalo was greater. He was drawn to don Chalo at just those times when the unresolved circumstances of his life were painfully present in his mind. And so he started up the mountain.

Just above the plaza, he passed don Luis' store. The old man, his silver hair parted neatly down the middle, stood smiling behind the counter. Don Luis was always fastidiously dressed in dark slacks, black leather shoes, a dress shirt buttoned at the neck, and, on cool days, a wool sweater. One of his sons was an engineer in Mexico City, and his daughter was married to a schoolteacher in Puebla. His store, like himself, was the cleanest and neatest in the entire village. Three men in soiled white clothing stood in the doorway to the store, talking with one another. Their muddy *pantelones* were rolled up above their knees, and the calves of their legs were coated with mud. The mud on their feet was so thick that it virtually obscured the *huaraches* that they were wearing. Don Luis waived a greeting to Celistino as he passed by.

Celistino's periodic discussions with don Chalo were a sort of compulsive ritual performed because of deeply rooted needs. Usually, he would describe and analyze his vision of the future of the village or lay out in detail some personal plan that he had been mulling over. Like many myths, his dream required this ritual reaffirmation in order to be sustained. Transforming them from vague mental images to relatively organized written thoughts, as he often did in his notebook, helped to give his dreams some concreteness, but actually to discuss them with someone gave them an even greater connection with reality, which not only sustained particular dreams but also sustained his entire approach to the dilemmas and conflicts that infringed upon his world.

He passed Alfonso Sanchez' house, the front of which served as a post office. Despite the new road, a mule was still used to carry in the mail twice a week. The mule standing in front of the post office had just been relieved of its heavy burden, and Celistino noticed the large, open sores on the animal's back. In the last few years there had been a noticeable increase in the amount of mail coming in and out of the village, resulting in ever-increasing loads for the mules. The sores were strange signs of the village's increasing connections with the outside world.

The street up to don Chalo's house was completely empty. Celistino did not seem to mind being alone in those last few minutes before he reached the chapel of the Little Virgin. He knew that don Chalo would either be at his post at the foot of the steps leading to the chapel or sitting at home. These two places and the cobblestoned path between them were just about the limits of his physical movements.

Celistino crossed himself as he passed the small cross and miniature altar at the base of the chapel. Fifty feet farther, and he had reached the foot of the stone steps. Don Chalo sat there quietly. His eyes were turned down toward the ground, but Celistino could not be sure what the old, blind man was seeing.

"Good afternoon, don Chalo," Celistino shouted. He always tended to speak loudly to don Chalo, as if his blindness made him deaf as well.

"Good afternoon, Mincho," don Chalo replied, referring to Celistino by his nickname. "Is it afternoon already?"

"It is two o'clock," Celistino said after consulting the sun.

"Two o'clock," don Chalo said incredulously. "Where does the time go?"

"You told me once that it doesn't go anywhere," Celistino reminded him, "but people just imagine that it does, and that is what makes them grow old."

Don Chalo laughed. "I think that I have too much imagination then, for I am growing old very fast. What brings you up here?"

"I was just passing by on my way to cut weeds for my pigs," Celistino replied. For some reason, he always tried to conceal the fact that he had come especially to talk with the old man. Perhaps it was to prevent don Chalo from feeling indebted, or, more probably, to prevent himself from feeling indebted to the old man.

"Is there no work today?" don Chalo asked.

"There are still a few ripe coffee beans, but the morning was very cold. It would not really have been worth it."

"Well, there are other things a man must do for himself. If he spends his time always looking for *centavos* he will miss something."

"What will he miss, don Chalo?" Celistino was smiling. Outwardly, he often seemed to be patiently humoring the old man, always on the edge of laughter and derision. But he kept coming back for more.

"He will be looking so keenly for such small things, like *centavos*, that he will never find the good life, and it will fall right past him."

Celistino laughed out-loud. "What do you mean by the good life, don Chalo?"

Don Chalo straightened up. "Look around you and open your eyes, and you will see." The words seemed strange coming from a blind man. "God has given you all of this, and you should never forget it."

"That is true, don Chalo, but one cannot afford to look around unless he has *centavos*. And it is a fact that today one must be looking for *centavos* constantly."

"One does not need to look for *centavos* when he has enough corn. Many years ago there was no need to look constantly for *centavos*, for then there was plenty of corn. The earth gave us a lot of corn when I was a young man. The Virgin was good to us." He pointed up the steps to the chapel. "She watched out for us."

"That all sounds very nice, but was it not a hard life? What good is there in being poor?"

"If you mean did we work hard, the answer is yes. But if you are asking if we then hated our life, the answer is no. As I have told you many times before, God gave the first people corn. For this reason, it is a good life. I cannot explain it further, but I know what I am saying. And as far as being poor, we did not lack anything. We had enough food for ourselves, and there were enough ways for the *centavos* to fall if one needed them. Too many people today have a lot of money, but they have become greedy and selfish. They keep everything for themselves and neglect God, the Virgin, and the saints. That is why the Little Virgin is making it so difficult for us. That is why the earth has said to us, 'I am tired. You don't give me the proper respect. I am tired.' We give them too little attention, and then they do the same to us. That is what makes some people truly poor."

Celistino and don Chalo were at a familiar impasse. Their conversations took many routes, but they all seemed to arrive at the same destination. Being familiar with their conversational cul-de-sac and aware that they had arrived once again, they both became silent.

Suddenly don Chalo stood up and started to throw his wares into a burlap bag. It was still early in the day, and on a nice afternoon like this don Chalo usually remained here much later. Celistino wondered where don Chalo was going and why he had so suddenly decided to leave. "Where are you going? It is still early," he said.

Don Chalo continued to toss the candles and religious trinkets carelessly into the sack. When he finished, he looked up at Celistino and smiled. "I have a good idea," he said, "why don't we go to my house and have a little *pulque** and honey to drink. A friend of mine just brought me a few bottles, and it is the best that you have ever had." Throwing the sack over his shoulder and picking up his cane, he started to walk toward his house before Celistino had a chance to reply.

Celistino just stood there and watched the old man slowly feeling his way up the path. Through all of their conversations, don Chalo had never once presented him with such an invitation. They had drunk coffee together frequently,

---

* A pre-Hispanic alcoholic drink made from the century plant.

but that was a formality in which even strangers at times engaged. But to share *pulque* and honey was much more intimate and significant, for even though the drink had lost the religious significance of earlier days, it was still considered by many *indios* as somehow distinct from other alcoholic beverages. And there had been an unfamiliar warmth in don Chalo's voice, which contrasted with the distance that he frequently tried to maintain.

Don Chalo was already fifty feet or so up the path. He stopped and turned back toward Celistino. "Come on," he shouted, "there will always be weeds for your pigs, but I don't offer my *pulque* to many people anymore." He turned again toward his house and continued walking. Celistino followed him.

They entered the house together, and don Chalo left the front door open to allow the fresh air and the afternoon light into the twelve- by ten-foot frame structure. Don Chalo hung the sack up on a nail and walked back into the cooking area. He reached behind the stone hearth and picked up a jar of thick, yellowish liquid and filled two large coffee cups.

"You will like this," he said as he handed one cup to Celistino, who was sitting in a wobbly wooden chair near the door. "It is part of the good life!" He laughed, and his eyes seemed to roll wildly in their sockets.

Celistino did not know whether or not to take him seriously. He accepted the drink and sipped it cautiously. The liquid seemed to leave a thick coating of sweetness from his mouth to his stomach. He had drunk *pulque* and honey before, but it had been many years ago, and he had forgotten the pleasant sensation of the liquid as it oozed slowly from the throat to the stomach. He took another sip, and his memory started to return.

"Very good," he nodded to don Chalo, who had already emptied almost half of his cup. "I can remember my father giving *pulque* and honey to me when I was just a boy living in Nauzontla. Of course, he usually drank *refino*, but I remember at times we would have this. Being sweet, it was a pleasant drink for a child."

"Yes, we used it as a special fiesta drink. The bottle would be passed, and everyone was obligated to pour a cup. Some people would have large jars or buckets, and if at some point during the night, they did not wish to continue drinking they would empty their cups into the large containers to take home with them. Some would empty cup after cup, but they were always obligated to take more." Don Chalo smiled contentedly, and both men sat there quietly for a moment taking long sips of the sweet beverage.

"My father used to say that this drink was sacred, and that a person must treat it as such." Don Chalo would have continued, but he somehow sensed that his companion had suddenly become saddened.

Celistino finished his drink and looked up at don Chalo. "I wouldn't know what that means anymore," he said. "For me, I must look for *centavos*—not sacred things—and I must hope that I am where they happen to fall. For me, that is all. You talk of goodness of corn, but what can that mean for me? I have no land. I can't grow corn out of my pores. My sweat and my blood come out of my pores, and still I can grow nothing. I do not own land, don Chalo, and because of this other men own me." The words were unusually strong for Celistino, and don Chalo appeared to be stunned to silence. He filled the cups again. Celistino took a deep breath and drank deeply from his.

"You, don Chalo," he continued, "you cannot live without your memories. Like this *pulque*, your past life lingers on in your mind long after you have consumed it. But me, I don't need memories. I wouldn't care if they faded forever." He paused to finish the second cup. "The problem is that no matter how hard I try, they never quite leave."

They sat there without saying a thing, both surprised at the intensity of Celistino's words. Ordinarily, Celistino remained dispassionate, giving almost mechanical descriptions of events and plans, always in control. This made his confession even more unusual.

The silence allowed Celistino to rechain his emotions. "This drink really is sacred," he said, pointing to the empty cup.

"Would you like some more?" don Chalo asked.

"Why not? There will still be weeds for my pigs tomorrow, and I know that if I leave now you will drink it all before the morning."

He stuck out his cup and don Chalo refilled it, emptying the glass jar in the process. "Don't worry, there is more." Don Chalo winked.

"Have I told you what I am going to do tomorrow?" Celistino asked rhetorically. "I am going to go down to Modesto Millan's house and make arrangements to rent the vacant *tendejon** that he owns. My family and I can live in the back and we can open up the front room for business."

He had known about the vacant *tendejon* for some time and had even recorded some tentative plans concerning its operation in his notebook, but he had never taken the initiative to investigate it further. Like so many of his other ideas, this one was not so much an actual plan as it was a myth that defended him against the memories that he could not quite leave behind. And dreaming the myth was a ritual springing not so much from his hopes for the future as from the disintegration of his past, a dam of external stoicism from which trickled mechanical discussions of positions and situations rather than an outpouring of true feelings and emotions. The dam had overflowed momentarily and become dangerously weak, but now it appeared stronger than ever. And so he talked of his plan. With the strengthening of Celistino's defenses against his emotionalism, don Chalo's temporary warmth had disappeared. A moment before, he had seemed to hear Celistino's every word, but now

---

* A small store which besides selling certain goods usually serves beer, soda water, coffee, and a few food items.

he sat quietly, immersed in his own thoughts. They sat there together, the one talking and the other listening but neither one hearing, both surrounded by dreams.

"That little store is in a perfect location," Celistino continued. "It is down at the lower end of town where the path that runs past the secondary school splits into two directions. The one on the left goes to Caxhuacan and the one on the right goes to Tuzamapan." He held his arms out to illustrate the fork in the path. "Do you know the place?"

Don Chalo did not answer. While Celistino had been talking, he had gone to get another jar of the *pulque* and honey and he filled their cups again. Celistino did not seem to notice.

"The store itself," he continued, "will give us steady money, and I can always still pick coffee beans if it is necessary. But the really good thing is the opportunity for commerce. And the secret is the location! Listen, the store is right in the middle of the fork. I will have the first opportunity to buy from people coming from Caxhuacan and Tuzamapan to the market here and the first opportunity to sell to them as well. And with the businessmen that I know in Zacapoaxtla, there is no telling where this might end. It will be no time at all, and I will never have to work in anyone else's mud again. And the key, don Chalo, is the location. Perfect!" He had already forgotten the painful memories and conflicts that had been resurrected that morning.

Don Chalo still said nothing. Slowly he placed his hand over his mouth to stifle a small laugh, but it was to no avail; the laughter came bursting out anyway. Celistino was puzzled. He had been talking about serious matters, and now don Chalo was laughing uncontrollably.

"What are you laughing at, don Chalo? What did I say?" The laughter was contagious, and Celistino chuckled slightly at first and then joined don Chalo in his hysterical fit of hilarity. They laughed for several minutes, and every time one stopped, the other seemed to laugh more hysterically until the other rejoined him. The sacred drink was beginning to work. Finally the laughter gave way to a few periodic chuckles.

"What was so funny, don Chalo? I was laughing without knowing why!" Celistino said.

"No, you said nothing," don Chalo replied. "As you were talking, an image came to me. That is what made me laugh."

"What was it?"

"Well, I could see the path splitting into two directions and the house placed right in the middle." He started to laugh again.

"And what else?"

"I could see two lines of people from Caxhuacan and Tuzamapan converging down the paths, coming closer and closer to a point directly in front of the house." Don Chalo paused to drink some more.

"I don't see what's so funny about that."

"I have not finished yet. As the people got closer I could see that they were carrying various things—vegetables, pottery, plastic things, corn, coffee beans, but mostly chickens." Don Chalo spat out the last word along with a bit more laughter that he was trying to contain.

"Chickens?"

"Yes, chickens, chickens everywhere. Big chickens, little chickens, fat chickens, thin chickens."

"Chickens?" Celistino asked again, beginning once more to laugh himself.

"Yes, yes, that is what I said—chickens. And they were all sleeping. Everyone was carrying the sleeping chickens, and more were standing asleep on everyone's shoulders and heads."

"But why?"

"It was market day. Brother, it was the biggest market day ever. And these two groups of people coming on the two paths were very, very quiet."

"Why?"

"They did not want to wake the chickens."

"Why?"

"Because it is easier to carry sleeping chickens, I believe."

"Exactly!" Celistino reached for the glass jar and emptied it into his cup.

"Now, at the very moment that the two groups were about to merge into the single path directly in front of the house, something startling happened."

"What?"

"You!"

"Me?"

"Yes, you. Suddenly, without warning you jumped from the front door of the house, screaming, 'Chickens! Chickens! Give me chickens!' You blocked their path and started grabbing chickens from them, stuffing them into bags and throwing them money in return." They both broke up laughing again.

"Can you imagine what the sleeping chickens did when they heard me scream?" Celistino barely managed to ask. "Then there were really chickens everywhere." Don Chalo laughed so hard that he fell out of his chair, and then they laughed at that.

They spent the remainder of the afternoon laughing, drinking, howling, and joking. No doubt, passersby were mystified by the loud sounds pouring out of the little house. But the *pulque* and honey had brought Celistino and don Chalo together as never before, and for that reason, how could one ever doubt its sacredness again?

Outwardly, they seemed so different. Years apart in age and differently attired, one as an *indio* and the other as a *mestizo*, they were nevertheless faced with the same general problems created by the changes in their world. Although they faced these changes in different ways—one retreating into memories of the past and the other hesitantly advancing into the future—there was a remarkable inner similarity. For they had both taken refuge in their dreams.

By late afternoon Celistino was feeling good. It had been a long time since he had last been so pleasantly drunk, and even longer since he had laughed so hard. With his feelings considerably elevated over what they had been only hours earlier, he finally left his companion. Instead of the usual friendly but formal handshake, they said good-bye with a series of not so steady embraces. Dark clouds had replaced the clear blue sky outside, and large drops of rain were beginning to fall. As Celistino walked toward the center of the village, he alternately whistled and hummed an improvised tune, paying little attention to the increasingly steady rain.

About halfway between don Chalo's house and the rock, Tlaloctepetl, he noticed an individual approaching the chapel. As the figure turned to climb the steps leading up to the entrance, he waved and shouted a greeting which Celistino promptly returned. Because of the sacred drink and since he was far away, Celistino had not recognized the man until he spoke. It was Ripolito Sanchez, a man about whom he knew very little. He watched as Ripolito hurried up the steps clutching a sheet of orange plastic around his shoulders to protect him from the rain. It was late and raining harder, and although happy, Celistino was beginning to feel the effects of the *pulque*. But something urged him up the steps and into the chapel behind Ripolito.

By the time that Celistino entered the chapel and tried to brush the rain from his unprotected clothing and dump the water that had collected in the brim of his hat, Ripolito was kneeling before the altar and the Little Virgin, some ten feet away. Celistino sat down quietly near the door on the only seat in the still incompleted chapel—a short plank held up by two cinder blocks. He propped his head up in his two hands and stared at Ripolitio and the altar.

The rain danced on the tin roof above them, dripping through small holes to stain the faded crepe paper that was strung from one wall to the other. Water ran slowly down the face of the rock which served as the wall behind the purple, plastic-covered altar. A steady drip splashed down on top of it and ran over the letters IHS carved on its front. At least fifty candles stood on the altar railings and on the floor, but only three were burning, and even they flickered weakly against the weather from which they were so ill-protected. The Little Virgin—warm, dry, and secure in her padlocked glass case—was surrounded by bouquets of silver-sequined pastel plastic flowers.

The first time that Celistino could recall having been there was almost twenty-five years earlier when he still lived in Nauzontla. His entire family, including his newborn baby brother, had made the difficult trip on foot. Being so young at the time, he was never told why the trip was made. He just remembered being tired, hungry, and somewhat frightened by the Little Virgin of whom he had heard his parents speak so reverently. His father had brought several ears of newly harvested corn to give to the Little Virgin as an offering of thanks for a good crop, but Celistino had always suspected that the trip had more to do with his baby brother than with corn. A few weeks after the visit, his brother had died, and his parents always maintained a silence about it.

After they moved to Jonotla, he had come here often with his father and several times with his mother. His father had continued to bring ears of corn to the chapel after each harvest, and, just before his death when he had no more corn, he had even brought a small pouch of the first-ripened coffee beans from the trees of his patron. Once Celistino and his mother went to the chapel shortly after moving to Jonotla, and he still remembered the surprise that he felt when his mother dropped the shawl from her head to reveal her short, shoulder-length hair. She had placed on one of the rock ledges to the side of the Little Virgin the nearly two feet of hair that she had cut off. He was never told the reasons for doing these things, but the fact that his parents had performed them faithfully and reverently indicated that they had been important. Over the years, his visits to the chapel became less and less frequent until now he rarely found occasion to come here.

Ripolito prayed on his knees for several minutes, and then moved around to the side of the altar where he stood

Altar in the Chapel of the Little Virgin

a few feet from the glass case, whispering inaudible prayers to the Little Virgin. He crossed himself and moved silently to the edge of the altar a few feet to the left of the Little Virgin. Stepping up on a small ledge several feet above the ground, he kneeled and prayed once again, only this time loud enough for Celistino to hear. His face stared directly into the solid wall of Tlaloctepetl and he prayed in his native language, Nahuatl. A few moments later, he reached into the *morral* that hung from his shoulders, removing something from the bag and placing it on another ledge above him. In another moment he was gone, nodding a silent good-bye to Celistino.

Celistino remained sitting and staring at the small glass case. Finally, attempting to stand, he fell forward on his hands and knees and crawled toward the altar, mumbling to himself. When he reached the altar railing, he pulled himself up and looked once again directly at the Little Virgin. Even that little bit of movement seemed to restore some sense of balance to his body, and he climbed up on the ledge where moments before Ripolito had prayed. Looking back into the small ledge above, he saw what Ripolito had left: four small kernels of corn. They were lying there on the natural altar formed on the side of Tlaloctepetl, along with a tiny bouquet of wilted white flowers, two sections of a beehive, four locks of hair, and a bundle of chicken feathers left by previous visitors to the chapel. And the sounds of Ripolito's prayer—the words of centuries past— surrounded Celistino like the dampness of the air, vibrating through his body like the rain pounding on the tin roof above him.

"Help us. Have mercy on us. Protect our cornfields from the winds and the rains as you did last year. Accept this corn, and through it make our fields provide us with a plentiful crop. Through you, *Nuestra Señora, Nuestra Mama-cita, Nuestra Virgencita, Madrecita de la Tierra,** we receive

---

* Our Lady, Our Dear Mother, Our Dear Little Virgin, Dear Mother of the Earth

everything. You are the guardian of our fields. We are the poor and we are helpless without you. Have mercy on us and give us our way and our life."

Celistino raised his head and released an agonizing scream which momentarily drowned out the pounding of the rain, the only other sound that could have been heard. When it was completely out of him, he slumped silently on his knees, resting his forehead against the rock wall. His voice seemed to linger in the air for a short moment, until once again there was only the sound of the rain.

Celistino did not return home that evening, but, instead, he went to the house of his friend, Ambroso, and they were soon moving from store to store, drinking small glasses of *refino* and chasing them with Orange Crush. They had not really behaved toward one another as friends for several months, and the need for that sort of companionship had swelled inside both of them to an almost intolerable level. A friend was not necessarily someone with whom one was completely open, but a person with whom one could experience a sense of stability and confidence in a largely chaotic and insecure world. Knowing that one could not have final victory did not discourage one from seeking the small temporary victories that could be had in friendship. It was simply the best that could be done. That was all.

Celistino had that day seen his defense dissolve for some reason, recognizing for a few moments that his dreams for the future were but shadows of his past. And when he had turned to see what forms were casting the shadows, there had been nothing there. So he did his best to forget what he had glimpsed about himself.

The future that Ambroso had chosen for himself was also being effectively undermined by his encounters with Pepe. He was attempting to create a new self-image by imitating the *macho*, but he was not well suited to the task, and his battles had only confirmed that fact. As a result, like Celistino, he had perceived something about himself that was too painful, if not impossible, to accept. So they were drawn together after so many months of being apart.

They drank that night with a special sort of abandon, marching from store to store with arms around one another, singing and laughing until they cried. They fantasized how they would both soon be rich and powerful and how, even if fate should somehow deny them their just reward, they were still each more of a man than anyone else in the village, and in the state of Puebla, and in all of Mexico, and in the entire world, and in the whole universe. From one dimly lit store to another they continued drinking and challenging their lot in life, in this way claiming a momentary victory for themselves. Perhaps the victory was only illusory like the honeybee that rejoices in its discovery of a pollen-filled flower only to discover too late that the "flower" is really a crab spider. But, perhaps, although short, the victory was also very real, for who knows the rules of the game or how the score is kept?

They were in don Luis' store for the second or third time. Who could really remember? They ordered two small glasses of *refino* and a bottle of Orange Crush. It was late, and they were the only people in the store except for don Luis, who was just as immaculately dressed and carried the same smile as he had when Celistino had passed by earlier on his way to don Chalo's house.

"I have this friend in Papantla," Ambroso began seriously, "and he has a friend in Tuxpan. And this friend in Tuxpan has a friend," and he paused to drink the *refino* and chase it with a sip of Orange Crush.

Celistino laughed as he completed the thought for Ambroso, "And this friend has a friend who has a friend who has a friend . . . and now we have established that you have a friend who has a friend who has a friend . . ."

"This is no joke," Ambroso interrupted. "Now, this friend of my friend in Tuxpan has a boat. A small boat, it is true, but nevertheless a boat. Listen. There is money in the sea!"

Celestino was laughing again. "Money in the sea?" he asked.

"Not real money, but *fish*, my friend. This man with the boat goes many kilometers out to sea, where there are millions of fish just waiting to get caught. In fact, I hear that they jump right into his boat."

"Why would they jump into the boat?" Celistino asked.

"Well"—Ambroso thought long and hard—"maybe they don't know how to swim!" They both bent over laughing. Don Luis smiled, waved his hand hopelessly, and disappeared into his living quarters behind the store.

"Are you afraid of the sea?" Ambroso finally asked. "Is it too dangerous?"

"If it is dangerous, then it is better! I like danger! I am ready to go to sea!" Celistino dramatically increased the volume of his voice with each phrase.

"Good, good. Tomorrow I will tell my friend that we are ready." They both finished the *refino* and shouted for don Luis to refill their glasses. The old man returned from the back room, and while he poured the clear alcohol he joked with the two men about their plans. They were so absorbed with themselves that they failed to notice a man who had entered the store through one of the several open doors. He stood there for a moment, smiling at the conversation that he overheard. Finally, folding his arms across his chest in a rather confident way, he abruptly interrupted them.

"Good evening," he said, "may I speak with you two men for a moment?"

"Whatever you like," Ambroso said, becoming serious once again. The man walked up to the counter and ordered a beer from don Luis.

"Do you know each other?" don Luis asked while opening the bottle of beer.

"I have seen you several times at Cornelio Luna's place, I believe," Celistino said tentatively.

"Yes, correct, correct. I have done some business with

Cornelio," the man answered. Don Luis then introduced José Perez, who was one of several men from Zacapoaxtla and Cuetzalan working in the village as a middleman since the completion of the road. These men usually established mutually profitable relationships with certain store owners in Jonotla, and together they would control the amount of goods that flowed into the various villages located further in the mountains. Since Jonotla store owners did not have the money to purchase trucks to transport goods to and from the village, and the wealthy outside commercial interests lacked the physical space and the connections needed to profitably establish themselves in the village, they came to depend on each other. So men like Señor Perez and Señor Luna became partners.

"I have a problem," Señor Perez said. "And as I was passing by, I heard you talking and thought that you might help me and at the same time I could help you."

Ambroso and Celistino looked curiously at one another. "What is your problem?" they asked in unison.

"Well, I am a businessman. And I have made a deal with a man in Huehuetla that I cannot now keep. I am having some temporary health and financial problems that will prevent me from completing the deal. But I am a man of honor and I have made an agreement, so I must find someone who can assume my responsibilities as well as the opportunities of the deal."

"What kind of deal?" Ambroso asked.

"Pigs," Señor Perez answered.

"Pigs!" Celistino laughed. "We are talking about becoming *fishermen*, a very dangerous business, and you talk to us about pigs! Who do you think that we are?"

"Two very intelligent men," Señor Perez replied immediately, "who know a good opportunity when it arrives. You can always become fishermen—there will always be fish in the sea. But these pigs will not be in Huehuetla forever. In a few days you can make good money and then do whatever you please. Are you interested?"

"Tell us everything," Celestino answered with renewed interest.

Señor Perez smiled and finished his beer. "This man in Huehuetla has twenty-five pigs, more or less, and he wants to sell them all for a very, very low price. He has agreed with me on the price, and I will send a signed letter along with you so that he will give you the same price. All you have to do is go and get them, bring them here to Jonotla, and sell them for a very good profit."

Celestino put his arm around Ambroso, and they conferred with one another over the proposition. Ambroso had managed to save close to 750 *pesos* from his work on the construction of the road, and Celistino said that he could get together the rest of the money. Ambroso was reluctant to use his money, since he had been painfully careful about saving it so that he might soon be able to move to a larger town and there find work. But they finally decided that the opportunity was worth the effort and the risk.

"We will do it," Celistino announced. Señor Perez bought them another round of *refino* and gave them the details of the deal and the name of the man in Huehuetla. Ambroso and Celestino went to bed that night with drunken anticipation of the next day.

It was still not quite light when Eudalia aroused Celistino from his deep sleep. "Wake up, wake up," she whispered, shaking him vigorously, "Ambroso is outside." Celestino heard the whistle greeting that Ambroso used to indicate that he was waiting. In a way, he was surprised that Ambroso was really there, for he could not even remember how he got home from don Luis' store. In fact, the details of the deal that they had received from Señor Perez were extremely vague in his mind, and he hoped that Ambroso would recall more.

"How did you tear your pants?" Eudalia asked, pointing out a large rip at the knee.

"I don't know. I think that I fell last night. I don't remember." Celistino was having trouble concentrating on anything.

"Where are you going so early?"

"To look for *centavos*," he replied as he stumbled out the door to meet Ambroso. Eudalia watched in silence as the two men disappeared in the darkness.

The trip to Huehuetla on foot was a difficult one over very rugged terrain, and it took Celistino and Ambroso most of the day to get there. The length and difficulty of the trip was not made easier by their hangovers, and when they finally arrived late in the afternoon, they had very little choice but to spend the night. They located the seller, closed the deal, and then retired early to a dilapidated vacant house. In the morning, they picked up the pigs—six grown ones and eighteen piglets—and were on their way back to Jonotla.

If they had thought the trip to Huehuetla was difficult, they had had no real idea of what the return journey held in store for them. The narrow, steep, and muddy path; the lush, dense vegetation that surrounded them on all sides; and the crossing of the Zempoala River made the trip arduous enough for two men on foot, let alone two men with twenty-four pigs. Driving the squealing, frightened, and unmanageable pigs in front of them, they fought a constant battle to keep them moving on the path and from getting lost. They had virtually to trot over the rough, muddy trail in order to keep pace with the fast-moving animals who would push unwary travelers off into the bushes or down the slopes that bordered the path. Often they had to plunge into the dense vegetation to retrieve one or more of their wayward companions, frequently getting scraped and cut in the process. By the time that they finally arrived in Jonotla—tired, hungry, dirty, cut, and bruised—the springtime sun was setting, and they had managed to lose four of their young pigs, although neither one of them knew exactly how or when.

Marching into the village, they passed directly in front of

the house that Celistino had excitedly described to don Chalo as having the perfect location for a store. He did not seem to notice, for he was engaged with a new dream.

The noisy entourage created a great deal of attention. Dogs barked furiously, making the pigs squeal and scramble even more; children laughed and pointed; and some adults stared in amazement while others shouted words of encouragement. Ambroso was enjoying the attention, waving and shouting to people who were stepping out of their houses to see what all the commotion was about. They lined the street like parade watchers, straining their necks to see, and pointing and laughing at the pigs, the dogs, and the two men who finally came into sight. Celistino, on the other hand, was doing his best to conceal his true identity. His hat was tilted down over his face, and he was walking with his eyes fastened on the ground—at least, as much as he dared risk keeping them there without stumbling or letting the pigs out of his sight. The absurdity of the entire scheme was fast settling in his stomach. The sale price in Huehuetla had certainly been good, but now they were four pigs short; they had had two very bad days; and they were being greeted with nothing but curiosity and good-humoured derision. It was a far cry from the respectability about which Celistino so often dreamed. He was supposed to be in a nicely stocked store with everything, including himself, clean and neat, dispensing information and advice about the operation, of successful business enterprises. But here he was in the streets, dirty and ragged, herding a bunch of uncontrollable pigs and dispensing nothing but his own embarrassment. Obviously, something had gone wrong.

At long last, they reached Celistino's house, driving the pigs straight through the front door and out the back door into the cement patio behind the house. Their journey completed, the two men collapsed from exhaustion and sat leaning against the back wall of the house. They watched in silence as Avencia ran excitedly through her now-crowded play area.

"Here we are," Ambroso finally said with a sense of disbelief. There were several minutes of further silence between them.

"Now, what do we do?" Celistino asked.

"I suppose that in the morning we will try to sell them."

"In the *morning*? Are you crazy? I don't want these pigs here all night! They are crazy! They will keep me awake! They will destroy my house! You keep them at your house if you love them so much!" Celistino was obviously tired.

"Celistino, you know that I have no place to put them all," Ambroso said in a tired but calm voice. "Where would they stay? In our house?" He managed a weak laugh.

Celistino looked at Ambroso. "I think that we should try to sell them tonight to don Vincente the pork butcher. We should have set up the sales before we went to buy the pigs, anyway."

"There was no time," Ambroso reminded him.

They went and spoke with don Vicente, but managed to secure only a promise that the *next time* he would be happy to do business with them. Discouraged, they walked out into the darkened street. "Where do we go now?" Ambroso's tone of voice suggested relief in just being home. "I think that I am going home to get some sleep," he answered his own question.

"No, no, we need to talk this thing over," Celistino said, grabbing Ambroso by the elbow and pulling him up the street. "Let's go to don Luis' to have a drink, and talk about what we are going to do tomorrow."

Soon, they were in don Luis' store drinking *refino* and Orange Crush and discussing possible contacts to be made in the morning. Although business was on their minds, it was not long before the *refino* replaced the pigs at the top of their list of priorities. As they drank more heavily, their discussion became increasingly pessimistic.

"I do not want much," Celistino said, "a small store, that is all. What we did the past two days is no better than working in someone else's mud. We are tired; we are sad; we

don't care; and we are still broke. And we may never sell
those pigs."

"Did I hear you say pigs?" came a voice from behind
them. There was a fat man leaning up against the counter
drinking a Pepsi. The man had been there for a while, but
neither Celistino nor Ambroso had noticed, so engaged
had they been with their own worries. "Excuse me," the man
continued, "I don't mean to interfere, but I believe that you
have been discussing pigs. Is that correct?"

"Yes, it is," Celistino replied.

"Good, good. Then what a work of fate this is," the man
said, crossing himself two or three times. "For I am looking
for some pigs to buy for a merchant in Cuetzalen. He doesn't
really need them, but he is always in the market, and I
would be glad to take them off your hands. For a reasonable
price, of course," he added.

"One moment, please," Celistino said, and he hustled
Ambroso off to one corner of the store. After conferring
for a moment, the two men returned to the counter. "We
have decided that since you are so hard-pressed for pigs,"
Celistino said, "that we will sell you our pigs, six grown fe-
males and eighteen—no, fourteen—small pigs at cost." Celistino failed to conceal a sly smile. He then proceeded to quote
a figure that was some twenty percent over what they had
originally paid for all *twenty-four* pigs.

The man finished his Pepsi and then laughed. "That is
more than I can pay," he said. "There is an oversupply of
pigs on the market now, so that prices are very low. But it
was nice talking to you." He put his hat on and started out
the door.

"Wait a moment," Ambroso said a bit overeagerly. "We
can come down in our price."

"Oh," said the man, "how much?"

"Two hundred *pesos*," Celistino replied without conferring
with Ambroso.

Ambroso turned toward Celistino and whispered, "Are
you crazy? Two hundred? You *are* crazy!"

The man turned and walked back toward Celistino. "It is a deal," he said, extending his hand outward. This time Celistino was ready with a firm grip to meet this stranger, and so the deal was closed.

The man paid cash, and with the aid of Celistino and Ambroso, he loaded the pigs onto a truck and drove out into the pitch-dark countryside. It had been less than half an hour since they had first met him.

"Come on," Celistino said as they watched the truck round the plaza and head down toward the road, "Let's go back to don Luis' for one more drink to celebrate."

"Celebrate?" Ambroso asked disbelievingly. "Why? There is nothing to celebrate! We only made maybe thirty-five *pesos*—seventeen and a half *pesos* each—for all that worry and all that work. We pushed those pigs over the mountains and nearly got killed for this? This won't even pay us back for the *refino* that we have drunk over the past several days." His voice was filled with disappointment, but still he walked alongside Celistino to don Luis' store.

"I know, I know," Celistino said. "But it is better this way. The deal was finished from the very beginning. I realized that when we came back into town tonight. We made a mistake, and it is better to forget it tonight than to carry it over until tomorrow. We should consider ourselves fortunate to have met this man."

As they stood there in don Luis' store having one last drink, Celistino reflected on the events of the past few days. It seemed as if everything had happened so fast; time was blurred, and events were blended. The *comandante*, the list of debtors, don Chalo, the *pulque* and honey, the visit to the chapel, Ripolito's prayer, the journey with the pigs, the list, the *pulque*, the prayer, the *comandante*, the journey—the thoughts would not cease their uncontrollable weaving in and out of his mind. His attempts to impose order on them were futile; the movement and pattern of his thoughts seemed to be governed by something outside himself. In a way, he wanted to give in to them, to allow them to jump and gyrate, but he was held back by a pervasive fear and loneliness that could not be shaken. In the midst of these memories of the past few days, blinking brightly like neon lights in his mind, he felt strangely certain of one thing: he was alone.

"Yes, my good friend, we were very fortunate that this man happened to pass by and overhear us," Celistino repeated, retreating into the safety of familiar words. "We would probably have been stuck with those pigs forever. It's funny how things like that work out by chance." He tried to smile.

"Yes, but the *centavos* did not fall," Ambroso said.

"Yes, but that is *life*, my friend." Celistino recalled the use of that word by don Chalo and Ripolito several days earlier. He turned to don Luis who stood behind the counter with that ever present smile across his face. "Do you know that man to whom we just sold the pigs?" he asked, realizing that they had never even introduced themselves to him or he to them.

"Yes," don Luis said, smiling, "his name is Lorenzo Betancourt. I thought that you knew him. He works with José Perez, the man who originally told you about the pigs."

"He is the partner of Señor Perez?" Celistino asked in astonishment.

"That is coincidental," Ambroso said.

Celistino breathed deeply and closed his eyes. "That was no accident," he said. "It was all planned. Perez and Betancourt got their pigs here cheaply and with no inconvenience to themselves. We were nothing but hired labor, and we didn't even know it."

They stayed there for another drink and then went home and slept long and hard. They had learned a valuable lesson, something to be remembered when in the future they went out looking for *centavos* again.

5–The Promised Land

Struggling upward from a deep crevice
past thick layers of rock discarded by time,
the summit lies just above, a sharp projec-
tile aimed and ready for flight into the
heavens where rainbow-hewn hopes soar
just beyond the senses. Upward, upward,
pushing past the silver and gold crystals
fused together by time. The summit is
there, one more step, one last stretch, one
great effort. And on a ledge below, a small
yellow flower smiles and bids farewell.

It was going to be one of those days. It was the hour of Wednesday morning Mass, and the church bells were not allowing anyone within a mile to forget that fact. The first metallic rings were like shock waves vibrating through the early morning calm. The sun was gamely trying to create the first dim shadows of the new day, and the old rooster outside Celistino's window was a bit ahead of his usual schedule. Celistino turned restlessly in bed, a fruitless combat with the forces that were interferring with a much deserved sleep.

"Celistino, get up! There is someone knocking on the door." Eudalia's voice suddenly joined the conspiracy. It was just over a week since the "Great Pig Deal," as Ambroso had come to call it, and Celistino had managed to find steady work, picking the last of the season's coffee beans.

He had worked long and hard for six straight days, and for the moment he wanted no part of the waking world.

Without lifting his head from the bed, he said, "Go see who it is. You need to go get corn ground soon anyway. Go on." He listened as his wife got up from the bed and fumbled around in the dim light for her clothing. Avencia was still sound asleep, curled up tightly against her father's back. A moment later, the creak of the door to the small front room in which they slept was followed by the scraping of the front door as it was opened. Eudalia's voice mixed with the familiar voice of a man, and then there was quiet until the bedroom door opened once again.

"Celistino, wake up," Eudalia said as she pushed on his foot. "It is the *comandante,* and he wants to see you immediately. He is in some kind of hurry."

"All right, all right." Celistino pulled himself out of bed and put his shoes on. "This Señor Arriaga must be crazy! He comes to *my* house before even the burros are awake and demands that *I* hurry! I'll tell him a few things!" He spoke more to himself than to Eudalia, and his words were not as much meant to threaten as they were designed to awaken him. He rushed to the front of the house and flung open the door, ready to question the necessity of such an early encounter.

"Ah, Señor de la Cruz, pardon me for disturbing you," the *comandante* immediately began. "I know that it is very early, but I have to catch the first bus to Zacapoaxtla. I will be gone several days, and I wanted to give you this money that I have collected for you before I left." He handed a folded wad of *peso* bills to Celistino.

"Well, thank you very much for your help," Celistino stuttered, forgetting his anger. Perhaps, it was due to his surprise over the speed with which the debts had been collected or to the money itself. Or, perhaps, it was simply the sight of the *comandante* and his recollection that he should behave as a proper sort of businessman. Or, perhaps, it was only Celistino. "I hope that you did not go to too much trouble," he continued, fingering the bills.

"No, no," the *comandante* said and laughed. "It is my pleasure to serve you. Of course, it was not without difficulty, but it is my job to uphold the law." He was serious again, and Celistino noticed that he was once more dressed entirely in black. "A few people resisted, but they will eventually pay their debts, or—" and he shrugged his shoulders in substitution for the obvious.

"Or, what?" Celistino cautiously asked. The possibilities raced through his mind—the *comandante's* large fists, jail, the white-handled revolver, or something worse.

"Ah, well, I am certain that we won't have to worry about that," the *comandante* replied. "People here seem to understand that the law is the law."

"I hope so."

"There were a few people who offered to give me chickens, eggs, corn, bananas, and all kinds of things in payment of their debts." Arriaga shook his head and grunted.

Celistino did the same, mimicking the *comandante's* combined amusement, disgust, and disbelief. He had become quite accomplished at slipping in and out of the roles that he imagined were expected of him, although his actions were often too stereotyped, giving them a kind of artificiality difficult to conceal. But if, as he frequently felt, he could not survive as himself, he would have to make it as he imagined others did, no matter how poorly conceived or inadequately carried out.

"Can you believe it?" the *comandante* asked.

Celistino shook his head again, adding a wrinkled nose to his response. "What did you do?" he asked.

"I could not take such things, that is certain. I explained to them that they must pay their debts in cash or not at all." He looked away and took a deep breath. "You do not want such payments, do you?" he asked, returning his gaze to Celistino.

"No, of course not," Celistino lied without hesitating.

"Can you see me carrying chickens, eggs, and all kinds of food around town?" the *comandante* asked.

"No, never," Celistino replied. He could have admitted that such a scene was not only quite easy but even irresistibly enjoyable to imagine. However, he valued his good health too much, and so he didn't deviate from the script.

"And can you imagine," the *comandante* continued in a tone of practiced incredulity, "how I would collect my twenty-percent fee? I have no use for a whole *chicken*, much less twenty percent of one!" And they laughed with one another, but not quite together, there in the first light of day, their shadows dimly outlined on the ancient cobblestones at their feet.

Celistino closed the door after Arriaga and went into the empty room, where he so often spent his time dreaming and planning. Eudalia had returned to bed and was sleeping soundly with Avencia. The morning was his alone. He unfurled the money and counted it out. There was a total of 118 *pesos*. Since the *comandante* had already subtracted his fee, this meant that around one third of the total debts had been collected. The amount would never make him wealthy, but it was worth three or four days' pay and could be used to pay off some of his own debts or to get him through the lean summer months that lay ahead. As he organized the money according to the denomination of each bill, he began to think that the *comandante* had been right all along and that his worries had been needless.

While still absorbed with the money, he heard another knock at the front door. Celistino tucked the wad of *pesos* into the front pocket of his pants and opened the closed shutters slightly until he could see who else was crazy enough to be pounding on his door at this hour. It was Ernesto Rivera, a man with whom Celistino rarely had any contact. Carefully closing the shutter, he wondered what in the world Señor Rivera would want with him, especially so early in the morning. Then he thought of a possible reason. Reaching into his shirt pocket, he removed the list of collected debts that the *comandante* had returned to him a few moments earlier. Running his finger down the list of names, he soon came to entry number six—Ernesto Rivera, thirty-one *pesos*. One of those abstract, lifeless names on the list was now pounding on his front door. Although he was reasonably certain of the reason that Señor Rivera was there, he was in no hurry to find out for sure. He rushed into the bedroom to wake Eudalia.

"Eudalia, wake up. There is someone at the door," he whispered.

She jumped up with a start and looked at him with a puzzled expression. He repeated himself. "Well, you are already up. Go to the door and see who it is yourself," she said, still puzzled.

"No, no, you don't understand! It is Ernesto Rivera! Do you understand? Ernesto Rivera!" He tried to maintain his whisper.

"Who?"

"Ernesto Rivera, the carpenter."

"Celistino, why can't you go to the door? What does he want?" Eudalia's voice was becoming louder and less patient.

"*Pssss,*" Celistino hissed, "not so loud. He will hear you." Eudalia sank back into bed. Celistino had never informed her of the reason for the *comandante*'s visits and she was, therefore, mystified by his present behavior. He sat down on the bed next to her. "Now, listen. This is very important. I want you to tell Señor Rivera that I am not here, and that you don't know when I will return. Do you understand?"

"But where would you have gone so early on this morning?" she protested. "To Mass? Ha! You never go to Mass anymore."

"I don't care what you tell him as long as you tell him that I am not here. Tell him you don't know where I am. Just hurry."

"Whatever you want, whatever you want," she said, finally

relenting. Standing behind the bedroom door, Celistino could hear them talking but could not understand what was being said. In a moment, Eudalia returned and, without saying a word, walked over to the bed and comforted Avencia, who was beginning mildly to protest being awakened.

Celistino stood motionless, waiting for Eudalia to report on her conversation with Señor Rivera. "Well, what happened?" he finally blurted out.

"I told him that you left before I had awakened and that I did not know where you had gone nor when you would return."

"Good, good. And what did he say?"

"He said that it was not very important that he see you today. He could come back another day." Eudalia's voice feigned lack of interest.

"Good, good. Did he say anything else?"

"He did say one thing as he left."

"What was that?"

"He said that I should tell you that he did not like to be treated like a criminal." Celistino's smile disappeared. Eudalia garnered her nerve. "What did he mean, Celistino?" she asked.

"Nothing, nothing. I don't know." Celistino leaned his back against the wall and put his hands into his pockets, touching the folded bills that he had placed there.

Eudalia stared at him for a moment. "Whatever he meant," she finally said, "you will have to talk with him sometime. You cannot hide forever."

"Yes, of course, I know. I just need some time to think."

"There is nothing more?" she asked, hoping one last time for some information.

"No, nothing more." As he turned to walk out of the bedroom, there was yet another knock at the front door. He froze in the doorway.

"I will see who it is," Eudalia said, knowing that she would be asked to do so anyway. Celistino stepped back into the room and waited. Only thirty minutes before, he had been sleeping safely with his family, unconscious of the existence of the forces which were prompting these sunrise visits. The *comandante* had given him a fairly substantial amount of money which, he would have to admit, was not altogether unwelcome—after all, it was really his to begin with. But he was still troubled. He had nothing against money, especially when it was his, but the whole idea of using the anonymity of the law and the alien person of the *comandante* to collect the debts disturbed him deeply. And then Señor Rivera had come obviously upset by the way he had been treated by Celistino. There was no telling who was at the door now. Perhaps it was a mob of debtors come to confront him and run him out of town. With these thoughts among the many which raced through his mind, he waited for Eudalia to return.

In a moment, he heard his wife's familiar voice accompanied by the voice of yet another stranger. He thought briefly about hiding, but instead he bravely stepped out to face his accuser. Perhaps it was not really his bravery, but only that there was actually no place to hide. To his surprise, the man he confronted was not an angry ex-customer and debtor, but instead a total stranger. He looked at Eudalia and then back at the man. "Who are you?" he asked.

The man seemed startled by Celistino's sudden appearance. "My name is Andres Sanchez," he answered, "and I am a friend of Señora Juárez. She asked me to come here for her."

"Oh? What does she want?" Celistino had always gotten along well with Delfina Juárez, the daughter of the patron who had been killed. She now owned the house and had graciously allowed Celistino and his family to live there for a modest rent. But he nevertheless expected the worst, and he was not to be disappointed.

The man smiled as those who want somehow to diminish the impact of bad news frequently do. Celistino noticed for the first time that he was carrying a large wooden rectangle under one arm. The man lifted the rectangle so that Celistino could see its white face and the neatly lettered black words upon it:

HOUSE FOR SALE.

30,000 *pesos*

SEÑORA DELFINA JUÁREZ

ZACAPOAXTLA, PUEBLA

"Señora Juárez has decided to sell this house," the man needlessly added. "The family has finally decided that they have no real need for it, and now that the road is finished and Jonotla is progressing so well, she is certain that they can sell it." The man paused as if waiting for a response. "I was passing this way," he continued, "and she asked me to put this sign up on the house. I was looking from the outside, and I believe that the upstairs window would be a good place."

"Yes, exactly," Celistino responded flatly, motioning the man toward the stairs in front of him. They all went upstairs, and Celistino and Eudalia watched as the man fastened the sign with some wire to the frame of the paneless window. When he had finished, he thanked them and bid them goodbye.

Celistino and Eudalia said nothing to one another. She went to prepare breakfast, and he walked downstairs and out into the street where he stood looking up at the newly placed sign. The sale price was more than he would earn in the next ten years if his present income could be maintained. If and when the house was sold, he and his family would have to relocate, most certainly in a smaller house. Although they lived essentially in a single room of the six-room house, the other vacant rooms did provide them with space that could be used for various useful purposes: for Celistino's reading and planning, for Avencia's playroom, or for Eudalia's laundry on a rainy day. They slept in one room and cooked and ate in another and made only rare and incidental use of the rest of the house, but still, it was

Celistino's house

much larger and nicer than they could afford normally. The large cement patio in back also provided ample space for Celistino's pigs. But more important than its convenience and modest, relative grandeur was the fact that the house was a part of Celistino's past. He had lived in it for over twenty years, and the debts of his parents and the patron, as well as a great portion of his security were inextricably bound up in the house. It represented an element of continuity between his present and past. The house was more than a place to live, for it was one of those few aspects of his past which were still a part of his present life. Such things were becoming increasingly rare. And now the reality of being forced to live elsewhere might serve as the final blow in effectively severing him from his past.

He stood on the street for several long minutes, as memories and less definable sensations and feelings raced through his body, and then he walked slowly back into the house to where Eudalia was preparing tortillas and beans. Avencia was sitting on the floor playing with an empty tin can. "I believe that I will go to Zacapoaxtla and talk to Delfina about the house," he said as he eased into an old straight-backed wooden chair.

"Why?" Eudalia replied. "She wants to sell, and we have no money. What is there to talk about?" She began the fast, rhythmic patting of the cornmeal into tortillas.

"I don't know, but I just think it would be a good idea to talk with her about it. Maybe we can work out a deal to stay here even if she sells it, or maybe she doesn't really want to sell it. I don't know, but I think that I should talk with her."

"Do what you want, but I don't see how anything can be changed." She paused to remove the first tortillas from the fire-heated stone hearth. "What about that house you told me about several weeks ago—the one down on the path to Tuzamapan and Caxhuacan? I thought that you liked that place and wanted to rent it. If you want that house anyway, there is no need to talk to Delfina."

"Yes, yes, but the house has already been rented to Luciano Millán. I did not check into it soon enough, and it was such an ideal place that it was rented very quickly. I did not move fast enough." Actually, Celistino had never investigated the availability of the house, and he had heard through the village grapevine that it had been rented.

"I must go to Zacapoaxtla," he concluded. They ate breakfast and did not discuss it any further. The next bus was due to arrive in Jonotla around noon. Eudalia and Avencia went to Mass, and Celistino spent the rest of the morning alone, thinking and feeding his pigs.

Shortly before noon, with a half-dozen tortillas Eudalia had packed in a *morral*, Celistino walked down to the northern end of the village on the roughly cobblestoned street that was soon to be paved so that the buses and other vehicles could roar right up into the center of the village. In places, the old cobblestones had been removed, and the wooden frames for the pouring of the concrete had been constructed. The road construction was already pushing beyond the village, although traffic could not presently go past Jonotla.

Celistino waited there with a handful of other people, and after a long while, the distant noise of the straining, old bus engine could be heard. It was amazing how far that noise carried in the cool, thin mountain air and how it seemed to consume all other sounds, especially those of the river, the insects, and the birds that normally filled the midday silence. This was to be Celistino's first trip on the bus since the road had been completed. Previously, he had made very infrequent trips to Zacapoaxtla, perhaps twice a year, and he had not been there since he had operated the store over a year ago. Although the road had eliminated the tiring three-hour walk to the highway, considerably reducing the difficulty of the trip, there was still rarely a need to travel, and so he stayed close to home.

Soon the bus was headed down the shoulder of Tlalocte-petl with its passengers, the engine straining in first gear to control the bus speed on the steep slope, brakes huffing and squealing, and the coach rocking back and forth, and up and down, as it encountered the many holes and small ditches that laced the road's surface. Celistino kept his eyes straight ahead, trying hard to avoid looking out the window. The narrow, shoulderless road clung to the side of the ridge overlooking the deep Apulco River valley, below the Chapel of the Little Virgin, and Celistino had no desire to admire the view. His hands gripped the seat in front of him.

In a few moments, the bus was at the bottom of the ridge, and the remainder of the trip on the dirt road was only bumpy and winding, lacking the panoramic views of the initial descent. Moving southeastward into the countryside, the number of coffee trees gradually diminished, and the sloping hills were increasingly covered with fields of corn.

until the highway was reached. Whatever fear was reduced in Celistino by the improved condition of the highway over the dirt road was rapidly turned by the increased speed of the bus. He had never become accustomed to the ride, and although it had been years since one of the aging buses had gone off the highway and over one of the many cliffs that lined it, he always sat tensely during the entire journey, until the bus reached his destination.

The trip from Jonotla to Zacapoaxtla covered a distance of only some twenty-five kilometers, although with the stops to pick up passengers and to refill leaking radiators, added to the driving conditions in the mountains, the entire trip took well over an hour. Despite his constant tension during the trip, Celistino could not help but anticipate his meeting with Delfina Juárez.

It had been almost ten years since Señora Juárez had left Jonotla with her family after the death of her father, and although Celistino had seen them numerous times when they had visited the village, he had never once visited them in Zacapoaxtla. They had joined the scores of families who mostly for economic reasons had left Jonotla for larger towns like Zacapoaxtla and for cities like Papantla, Poza Rica, Tezuitlan, Puebla, and Mexico City. The increasing economic pressures in the village, as well as the aspirations of recently graduated students from the six-year primary school and the three-year secondary school, had significantly increased the flow of people from Jonotla. The discouragement and frustrations created by these pressures and unfulfilled aspirations combined with the mythical lure of the promised land to both push and pull Jonotecos from their village. Most of the people migrating from the village to the "oases amidst barren deserts" were motivated both by despair and by hope. But as promised lands always have been, these, too, were based on largely false hopes, a fact which many people understood. And, yet, it didn't diminish their desire to search out these promised lands, for even false hope is infinitely more tolerable than no hope at all. And so they continued to leave.

There was a noticeable absence in the village of young people, young men in particular, in the age-group of twenty through thirty-five. Actually, the population showed a decline beginning at about age fifteen, but it increased dramatically in slightly older age-groups. Some young men would return to resettle in the village once they inherited parental lands, but most were gone forever, living in the promised lands of urban slums.

As the daughter of the man who had once done so much for his parents and later for him personally, Celistino had always admired Delfina. She was several years older than Celistino, and, although there had always been some distance involved in their relationship that was imposed by their fathers' relationship, he had many fond memories of their childhood together. Then, whcn she was seventeen, she had married a man who was thirty. The man owned five or so hectares of coffee trees, was a part-time carpenter, and, after their marriage, helped to manage his father-in-law's fairly substantial landholdings. By village standards, they were a very fortunate and highly successful family.

But their success did not insulate them from tragedy. After her father's death, Delfina experienced a sense of despair that was difficult to overcome. Although she inherited the house and a few other things, her two brothers received all her father's land, and it was not long before she and her husband made the decision to move to Zacapoaxtla. Unlike most of the other migrants, they were not pushed from the village by economic necessity, for she and her husband possessed ample resources to maintain themselves at a higher-than-average standard of living. Their landholdings of slightly more than five hectares was greater than almost ninety percent of the other village landowners, and their income from the sale of coffee was supplemented by his work as a carpenter. But even though they were motivated more by a despair that had its source in her father's death and in a hope that originated in a desire to leave behind painful memories than they were by economic pressures, they still had left for Zacapoaxtla with the same sort of longing for deliverance with which the others had departed. The lure of the promised land stretched before their eyes.

Although Celistino knew little about the Juárez family's current situation, he vividly imagined their success. That image reaffirmed his own promised-land dreams, and he was alternately attracted to and repelled by it. Sometimes he rejected it, because it created the despair that swells inside when one witnesses others taking the giant stride that one fears too much to take for oneself. He needed his dreams, but he also needed them to be sufficiently isolated from reality to insure that they always remained dreams.

Celistino was certain that Delfina and her family had found the promised land. They had left Jonotla as a very successful family, and the opportunities in Zacapoaxtla would guarantee their good fortune. When they left, Señor Juárez had been promised a job as a carpenter, and Celistino was sure that by now he was running his own business, perhaps, in building supplies. Zacapoaxtla was the commercial center for a wide area of the Sierra Norte de Puebla, a town with approximately four thousand people and with a hundred or more stores, as well as numerous businesses that shuttled goods in and out of the region. In such an environment, Celistino was certain that someone with the resources of Señor Juárez could not help but become wealthy, important, and happy. After all, even he, Celistino, would manage that much when he made the move at just the right moment in the future.

In a way, the bus ride and the anticipation of meeting Señora Juárez and her family was like a trip through time into the future to meet his own dream fulfilled. The old bus bounced around the curves and strained up the hills, stopping to load on more passengers going to the market in Zacapoaxtla. Soon all of the seats were occupied, and the aisle was packed so tightly that one person could hardly move without everyone moving. It was the sort of public closeness that brought about a silence that seemed misplaced among so many people. No one spoke, and the only sound was the roar of the engine. The passengers quietly swayed and bounced along with the old bus toward their destination.

Finally, a man who was standing against the seat in which Celistino sat turned and spoke to him. "Are you going to Zacapoaxtla?" the man asked. Celistino could barely hear him above the engine.

"Yes, yes," he answered, "and you?" Celistino recognized the man as a resident of Jonotla, but he could not recall his name.

"Yes, I am going on business to buy a few things. Why are you going?"

"I am on business, too. I am here to visit Señor Gildardo Salazar," Celistino replied, referring to Delfina's husband. "Do you know him?"

"Did he use to live in Jonotla?" the man asked. Celistino nodded. "Then I know him," the man said. "He and his family moved to Zacapoaxtla years ago, did they not?" Celistino nodded again. "Then I know them," the man continued. "How are they? What is Señor Salazar doing in Zacapoaxtla?"

"Oh, he is in business for himself. He has a store as well as other commercial interests," he replied, not from any knowledge of Señor Salazar's work, but from his hopes and dreams. Gildardo and Delfina had always done well in Jonotla, and he was certain that it would be the same in Zacapoaxtla. The bus suddenly screeched to an unexpected halt, and the people who were standing fought to keep their balance. Celistino glanced out the window and at eye level saw nothing but clear blue sky. Shifting slightly, he looked out and down and saw that the bus was stopped in the wrong lane on the edge of the pavement with about a two-foot shoulder separating it from a thousand-foot drop into the green valley below. Looking quickly back into the center of the bus, he reinitiated the conversation.

"What is happening?" he asked.

"I don't know," the man answered. "I can see another stopped bus directly in front of us, but who knows why?"

In a moment, the bus lurched ahead and pulled back into the right lane and continued down the highway. There had been a small rock slide covering the right lane, and the driver of Celistino's bus had tried to make it around the slide despite the oncoming bus, assuming that the other driver would stop to allow them to pass. Instead, the other driver had taken up the challenge, and the two buses had raced toward one another, each daring the other to yield. Not until it had become apparent that neither was going to give in did the two drivers slam on their brakes. As it was, everything turned out all right, but it was because of this sort of thing that Celistino wished that he was back in his room reading his illustrated dictionary.

By the time that the bus pulled into the plaza in Zacapoaxtla, it was already midafternoon. The town appeared to be larger than it actually was. Signs of its relative prosperity as a market center were everywhere. The main streets were all paved, in good repair, and unusually clean. The houses and stores which lined the narrow streets were uniformly in good condition, and it was obvious that their plastered exteriors were regularly repaired and painted. The plaza was clean and well kept, with a small fountain in the center surrounded by walkways, benches, and greenery. Well over a hundred stores of various kinds lined the streets. In fact, it appeared as if almost everyone who lived there had some sort of store, most of them located in open-front rooms of their houses. The main church, although it was centuries old, had a large clock in its bell tower which chimed every fifteen minutes. Cars and large flat-bed trucks, many of them new, roared up and down the streets. In the entire *municipio**

---

* Similar to a county

with a population of just under twenty-one thousand people, over 75 percent of the land was owned by only 3½ percent of the landowners, most of whom resided in the town of Zacapoaxtla.

On market days, the hustle-and-bustle and prosperous appearance of the town was intensified as the daily food market overflowed its housing into the main streets, where peddlers in stalls sold everything including clothing, plastics, prepared food, and tools. Trucks filled with diverse marketable items lined the streets and alternately loaded and unloaded goods on the way in and out of the town. Buses, taxis, and trucks, carrying as many as five thousand buyers and sellers from the numerous smaller communities surrounding the town on a single day, kept up a steady stream of traffic. It was obvious on any day, but especially on market day, that there was great wealth in Zacapoaxtla. To a person from a small village where streets were mostly mud and cobblestones, where houses were neglected and unrepaired, and where the plaza was old and decayed, it was easy to see how this town could be impressive, especially if that person held commercial activities in high esteem and could not see beyond external decay to the fast fading strengths beneath.

Celistino wandered through the streets, stopping now and then to examine items with which he was not entirely familiar—can openers, plastic fruit juicers, tortilla presses, and rolling pins. There were stalls selling more familiar items like sarapes, *huaraches*, *machetes*, and pottery, but he paid little attention to these. They were things that he had seen all of his life, so why bother with them now?

Surrounded by the market-day splendor of Zacapoaxtla, he almost forgot the reason why he had come. Not knowing where the family lived, he decided to ask directions of one of the several food vendors located near the bus stop. He walked up to an elderly woman who was roasting ears of corn over coals.

"Yes, yes, tell me how many you want," the lady de-

An elderly indio *couple at the market*

manded as she reached to pluck one of the ears from the grill.

"Ah, just one," Celistino replied. He was not really hungry, but for some reason he already felt indebted to the woman for the information that he hoped to attain from her. He seemed to feel uneasy and alienated in this environment. He wanted to feel as if he belonged, and he wanted others to feel the same. And so he bought the corn.

He stood there with one hand in his pocket, trying hard to appear blasé about the scene around him, and took several bites from the steaming ear of corn. After a moment, he turned back toward the old lady and asked, "Do you know where Señor Gildardo Salazar lives?"

"Who?" she asked, straining to hear over the noise of a nearby bus that was starting its engine.

"Señor Gildardo Salazar," Celistino shouted.

"No, no, I don't know him. Are you sure that he lives here?"

"Yes, yes. He is a carpenter, and I believe that he might have a store. His wife's name is Delfina Juárez, and they have four children. Are you sure that you don't know them?"

"No, I have never heard of them, but you might ask at Justo Caldera's store. They know everyone who lives here." She pointed across the plaza to a corner store with large lettering above the door, reading "Justo Caldera, S.A." Celistino knew that the Caldera family was the wealthiest family in the area. They owned several of the largest stores and both of the hotels in Zacapoaxtla, as well as a great amount of municipal land and other commercial interests. The name Caldera was written across store fronts and commercial trucks throughout the town. Celistino felt certain that the Caldera family would know where to find a fellow businessman. It was true that Señor Salazar had only been here for about ten years, while the Calderas had been in the area for almost two centuries, but, nevertheless, they were both together in the world of commerce, and, perhaps, in another century or so, the name Salazar would attain a prominence equal to that of Caldera. Celistino was convinced that this would be the case.

He walked across the plaza past stalls of blue and pink plastic sandals and brightly colored plastic wares. The store was crowded with people examining various objects. Making his way toward the counter, Celistino decided to ask an elderly woman who was sitting behind the counter for directions. She was the least busy and, for some reason, appeared easier to approach.

"Excuse me," Celistino began, "but I would like to ask if you know Señor Gildardo Salazar, or his wife, Señora Delfina Juárez?" He smiled, waiting for a response. The old woman just sat there, staring straight ahead. Celistino glanced around the room nervously; he was beginning to feel awkward. He did not enjoy feeling like a stranger, and asking directions always made him feel as if he were one. No one in the store had seemed to notice. Turning to the old woman again, he repeated the question. Still, there was no response, no movement which even minimally acknowledged his presence. While he stood there, trying to understand what was happening and what he might do about it, he felt a light tap on his shoulder. Turning, he saw a short lean man in his mid-forties standing there, smiling at him.

"Excuse me, señor," the man said in an even voice, "but my mother can neither see nor hear. It is her age, you know. Would you believe that she is over eighty years old?" The man took his mother's hand in his, and the old woman broke into a wide grin. Celistino was relieved that her silence had been nothing personal. "My name is Justo Caldera," the man said, thrusting his hand out vigorously. "Now, how can I help you?"

"Well, I am looking for a friend of mine whom I have not seen for a number of years," Celistino replied. "He and his family moved here from Jonotla ten years ago, and I don't know where they live."

"What is his name?"

"Gildardo Salazar, and his wife's name is Delfina Juárez. They have four children, I believe. He was a carpenter and a businessman in Jonotla, and I am certain that he has a store here. If you don't know where he lives, perhaps you could tell me where his store is located."

"Gildardo Salazar, the carpenter?" the man asked. "Yes, I know him. He has done some repair work for me, and he is a fine carpenter."

Celistino nodded in agreement with the compliment given his friend, but Señor Caldera's voice had a condescending edge on it, and it made Celistino uncomfortable. "That is good," he said. "Then you can give me directions to his house or to his store." His voice wavered between a statement and a question.

"Yes, to his house, but to his store, no." Señor Caldera shrugged his shoulders and laughed.

"Fine, how do I get to his house?" Celistino listened as the directions were given to him. At that moment, he was not feeling particularly confident. The nervous anticipation of seeing Delfina and Gildardo in their situation in Zacapoaxtla made him uneasy. And Señor Caldera's condescending laugh had added to his confusion. The promised land of his imagination was much more agreeable than reality.

As he followed the directions to the house, his imagination created various images of Delfina and Gildardo's life in Zacapoaxtla; he imagined a newly constructed, two-story white house, small balconies with black wrought-iron railings filled with colorful flowering plants—mostly geraniums which he had read about and seen only in his illustrated dictionary; neat, well-furnished rooms; a small interior patio, open to the sky, and filled with every imaginable sort of luxurious growth that the semitropical mountain climate could sustain, including banana trees bent to the ground by the weight of their fingers of gold; and finally, the smiling faces of Delfina and Gildardo next to their four clean, happy, and well-mannered children. It was a still life of domestic bliss, an image so lifeless that even Celistino might have doubted its authenticity. But he persisted in seeing it, as if he believed that if he could somehow maintain the serenity of their life in his expectations; then he would be able to accept a lesser life style, if need be. Perhaps, the house would be smaller, and maybe there would be no banana trees, and everyone has some problems; they can't smile all the time. Not even in the promised land.

The directions given to him by Señor Caldera took him southward, away from the center of town. Here the noise and excitement of market day were gone. The streets were quiet and empty. Occasionally, out of the corner of his eye, Celistino would notice a shadowy figure peering out from the dark interior of one of the houses that he passed. Otherwise he saw no one. The paved street turned to dirt, and the houses were noticeably smaller and less well kept than those closer to the center of town. The neat, white-plastered exteriors became unfinished, unpainted planks, as the prosperity of the town seemed to have been left several hundred yards back toward the plaza. Increasingly, the area that he was passing through seemed to be a strange location for the dream house of his imagination. He stopped several times to check the accuracy of the directions that he had received, drawing some of those obscured faces out into the light of day. "Straight ahead," he was told once and then again. Finally, he was told that it was straight up the hill, third house on the left.

By this time, he realized that something was drastically wrong. As he walked, he braced himself to receive the jolt that was now certain to come. In a moment, he stood in front of the third house on the left. It was a small, single-room stone-and-plaster structure, not at all unlike most of the houses in Jonotla. There were several chickens pecking about skittishly, and a scrawny dog, its ribs protruding like latticework beneath its skin, was sleeping near the open door. A three-year-old girl appeared in the doorway, barefoot and dressed in an undersized, tattered white dress, staring curiously at Celistino. There were no balconies, no wrought iron, no flowers, no patio, no banana trees. He feared that there would be no smiles either.

As he neared the door, the child disappeared into the house. "Good afternoon," he shouted, turning away to await the response.

"Yes?" came a soft voice from inside the doorway. Celistino turned and saw Delfina standing there; her wrinkled brow and squinted eyes indicated a struggle to see clearly out into the bright sunshine.

"Celistino!" she shouted, "Come in! Come in!" She was smiling broadly. "Sit down, sit down! What are you doing here in Zacapoaxtla?" She was obviously surprised and happy to see him. Her smile seemed to envelope her entire face, and made her appear much younger than she actually was. Her thick wiry black hair hung loosely and bushed-out around her small, dark face. Celistino stared at her.

"What are you doing here in Zacapoaxtla?" she repeated.

"I was just passing through," he said, knowing that it would be better to wait with the real explanation, "and I thought that I would come to visit you."

"I am happy that you did. Will you be here long? If you need somewhere to stay, you are welcome to stay with us." She was still smiling.

"No, no. I am just here for a few hours," he said. As he talked, he glanced around the single room. Against one wall there were two double beds, one probably used by Delfina, her husband, and the three-year-old, and the other by the three older children. Against the opposite wall was a small table, and there were five or six straight-back chairs scattered about the room. Along the back wall, near the doorway that led into the partially enclosed cooking area, was an old Singer pedal-operated sewing machine and a large trunk. There was no other furniture in the small room. It was hardly what he imagined their life in the promised land would be, but at least she was smiling.

"It has been a long time since you have visited Jonotla," he said. "How have you been?"

"Very good, very good," she replied. "We like it here in Zacapoaxtla very much. It is not as cold here as it is in Jonotla, and the wind does not seem to blow so frequently or so hard." Her smile faded as she spoke, and she tried in vain to rescue it as she finished the last sentence. She had answered a question about herself in terms of the weather, and the emptiness of her words seemed to fill the room with clouds of emotion. "Oh, there have been the usual problems," she continued once she had regained her smile. "But that is life."

"Yes, that is life," Celistino repeated. As well as anyone else, he understood what she meant. For life has its problems, and in those long stretches between good times, one wonders when things will equal out. It is like watching the nights grow longer and the days shorter as winter approaches, without being certain that the longer days of spring and summer will ever come.

There was a long silence. "Where is Gildardo?" Celistino finally asked.

"He is working," she answered, without offering additional information concerning the nature of Gildardo's work. Having had one important image shattered, Celistino needed new information with which to reconstruct his dream world. Delfina and Gildardo were two people linked closely to his past, especially those moments, now shaded by time, which had gradually dislodged him from that past. And so they were inextricably bound up in the web of his life, faded forms of familiarity cast headlong into the unknown world of a time fast approaching. There was no way that he would just stand by and allow them and the promised land simply to disappear from his dream world.

"What kind of work is he doing now?" he asked, his voice becoming louder, as if he were really demanding an explanation for the destruction of that house and the elaborate fanciful dream that he had constructed.

Delfina's smile disappeared once again, "When we first came here, he worked as a carpenter," she began.

"Yes, I know that," Celistino said rapidly, prodding Delfina to hurry past the unnecessary preliminaries.

"Well, he did quite well at first," she continued. "There were several new houses that he helped to build and some furniture orders that helped. He even thought that he would be able to open a store and sell tools and various other kinds of things. We had a stall in the market for a while, selling hammers, saws, *machetes*, and other things. It was the beginning, you know?" She looked at him for some kind of understanding.

Watching her, he had momentarily forgotten about himself. "Yes, I know," he said softly.

"But then the jobs just stopped coming and no more *centavos* fell. So now he does various kinds of jobs."

"Carpentry jobs?"

"Any kind of job." She managed a laugh. "Carpentry, field work, repair work, road work—any kind of work. And I do some sewing," she said, motioning toward the old sewing machine.

Celistino got up from the chair and walked around the room. He seemed to be searching for the right words. "But what about the store and the house and the other things?"

Delfina looked puzzled. "What store and house and other things?"

"The things that you came here for," he said in a forcibly restrained voice. He was doing his best to control the feeling of abandonment that he was experiencing. Delfina and Gildardo had failed to live up to his expectations, leaving him alone with a partially hollow dream, and he seemed both angry and disillusioned.

"Celistino, I came here more to escape something than to find something," she reminded him. "It is true that we had plans and hopes, but what has happened is God's will, and I am certain that things will get better." She appeared to possess a genuine sense of hope combined with a solemn, resigned contentment. Many of her dreams about the promised land had been broken, but at least those painful reminders of her father's death had been left behind in Jonotla.

Celistino stood quietly by the door watching the three-year-old child play with a stick in the dirt. Delfina stared at his back. "Celistino, what is the matter?" she finally asked. "It is our life, not yours. So why are you so concerned?"

"I just thought it would be different—that is all," he said, turning toward Delfina and smiling. "It is not important. It is not important." But his words were unconvincing. The reality of Delfina and Gildardo's life would forever quake and quiver just beneath the surface of his dreams.

It was obvious that Delfina had come to accept her life in Zacapoaxtla. For better or for worse, she was busy living out her life, the bad along with the good, the difficult along with the easy; but Celistino, having elevated Delfina and Gildardo above the world of real people in an effort to somehow strengthen the crumbling fortresses in his own mind, could not just accept what he saw. The reality that he had confronted continued to trouble him.

"How are things in Jonotla?" she asked, trying to end the painful silence that filled the room and, at the same time, to imprison Celistino's feelings in conversation.

"Fine, more or less," he replied. "Things are pretty much the same as always. There is not much work now, but there were a lot of coffee beans this year, and so there was a lot of work during the season. In fact, there was too much!" He sank into the chair with mock exhaustion, and he and Delfina laughed long and hard. For the moment, they had managed to focus on less troublesome things. They were safe.

"Eudalia and Avencia are fine, too," he continued. "Avencia is getting bigger and bigger all the time, and I am, too," he said, patting his stomach. And they laughed again.

"You still laugh like a little boy," she said. "It is a sound that brings back many memories."

"Yes, I suppose that it does." He was beginning to show signs of being troubled once again.

"Do you remember our first adventure together, Celistino?"

"Let me think. Was it the time that we let Señor Prado's pigs loose in the streets during a hard rain?"

She laughed. "No, no, it was much earlier than that, although that time was one of our best."

Celistino thought hard but could come up with no more suggestions.

"It was shortly after you moved to Jonotla—you must have been around eight years old, and I was around twelve—and you were working with your father in my father's fields," she said. "Do you remember?"

"Yes, I think so. Keep talking."

"Well, I rode out with my father on his horse to the fields, and when it was time to go, I wanted to stay. Do you remember?"

"Yes, it is very clear. I remember."

"So my father asked you and your father to watch out for me and to bring me home when you were through working. I remember that he kept asking me whether I was sure that I wanted to walk home rather than ride. And I was so certain that I did."

"As I recall, it was more than an hour's walk, mostly uphill," he said, shaking his head as if he was struggling with the climb at that very moment.

"Yes, it was more like an hour and a half. Anyway, your father decided that he wanted you to go home early for some reason—I forgot exactly why . . ."

"I do not remember, either," he interrupted.

"And I decided to walk home with you." She was smiling, anticipating the story's end. "So we went walking down the path together—you were carrying a large, heavy bundle of firewood." Celistino winced, remembering, and rubbed his shoulders in mock pain. "Since the trail ran through the river valley, it was very narrow and surrounded by dense growth." Celistino visualized that spot—it was not only covered with thick ground cover, but the dense trees formed a ceiling of green, which filtered out a great amount of the sunlight, even on a bright day, and the songs of myriad birds and insects resounded throughout the woods.

She continued, "Well, it seemed that you thought that I knew the way home, when I was really not sure at all. I had made the walk a couple of times before, and I thought that I knew, but when I got down into the valley forest, where one can barely see the sky, and the familiar mountains not at all, I was lost."

Celistino laughed. "And I remember," he said, still laughing, "that you thought that I might know the way home, but I was as uncertain as you."

"We must have been lost for several hours. We were hungry, tired, and dirty—I believe we both must have fallen down twenty times. Finally, we sat down to wait, for what I am not sure. Perhaps, only to regain our strength. We had been climbing up out of the forest to get a clear view of the surrounding mountains, but every time that we went back into the woods, we would again lose our way." They both sat there smiling and shaking their heads at their memories.

"Then we heard a voice in the distance calling for us, and we ran and ran until we met with that voice. It was your father. We were certainly happy to see him. And he led us home," Delfina concluded.

They talked and laughed for another hour or so, mostly about warm memories that touched a deep chord within them both. But despite the external warmth, there was an underlying chill and formality, partly due to custom, but partly due to individual memories resurrected but not shared. It was no meaningless accident that Celistino had come with the expectation of meeting his future, but had instead found himself wrapped in memories of his past. The future that he had encountered was not at all what he had imagined, and so the past seemed like the only place that he could comfortably go. Delfina and Celistino had somehow realized this simultaneously, and they spent the afternoon together with their past.

It was not until later, as he walked slowly back to town, that Celistino remembered he had forgotten to talk to Delfina about the house in Jonotla. He thought about returning to ask her about it, bringing a slight hesitation to his stride, but he decided to continue.

He had come with the hope of receiving some sympathy for his own situation, but he had ended up giving rather than receiving it. He was confused by his feelings. Certainly, the compassion that had run through his body as he spoke with Delfina had been genuine enough, but it had been mixed with feelings of resentment, as if the emotions generated in him somehow deprived him of the sympathy that was rightly his. The feelings of sorrow for Delfina that he had experienced while sitting with her seemed to diminish with every step. He had left her, and at least for now, he was no longer emotionally burdened by the look on her face or the sound of her voice. Her presence had seemed to demand the gift of his compassion, but now that he was out in the street alone, his sense of sorrow had been redirected toward his own dreams. There was simply no way that he could leave himself behind.

Soon, he had returned to the center of town, where the market was just as bustling as when he had left. There the noise and commotion captured his attention as he walked from one stall to the next, looking at and occasionally touching the myriad items that were still relatively novel in the world of Jonotla, but which could easily be incorporated into his dreams.

He purchased another ear of corn and walked through the streets, trying to regain his confidence by speaking with vendors and others as if they were old friends, and striding along as if these surroundings had been his since birth. Within an hour, he had spent almost all of the money that he had brought along with him, which was, indeed, almost half of what the *comandante* had collected for him.

He bought a pair of metallic blue plastic sandals and a yellow plastic juicer for Eudalia, a big green ball and a pink flowered dress for Avencia. For himself, he purchased a new straw hat. His old hat had been small-brimmed and flexible; the new one had a slightly larger brim that was stiff and curled upward, like the smile that he had fixed upon his face. The new objects massaged his spirit; they enabled him to look contentedly outward rather than painfully inward.

By the time the last bus returning to Jonotla left, the last light of day was giving way to darkness. The buildings, people, and few remaining stalls appeared like immobile shadows out the window of the fast-moving bus. The window seemed to frame in Celistino's mind these last glimpses of the promised land. As the bus roared out of town and into the countryside, the high mountains to the west were capped by the last glimmers of the setting sun. Celistino watched as the color of the horizon changed from pink to red to purple and, finally, to the encompassing blackness of night.

The bus made its way toward Jonotla, stopping at virtually every little side road to unload passengers. All the seats, as well as the aisle, had been filled with people when the bus left, but now—half an hour later—there were only a few people still standing. Celistino sat quietly staring out the window. He tightly clutched the *morral* that was filled with the items that he had purchased. He remained uninterested in, even oblivious to, his immediate surroundings.

Suddenly, as if awakened from a deep, dream-filled sleep, he was jarred by the voice of the bus driver shouting, "Nauzontla! Nauzontla!" The driver had shouted the name of every one of his previous scheduled stops, but Celistino had not really heard any of them until now. "Nauzontla . . . Nauzontla" . . . the name ricocheted through his mind. It was the town of his birth, and the voice of the driver coming from the darkened front of the bus seemed to be calling him home.

Without thinking, he jumped from his seat, stumbling

over the feet of the man who was sitting next to him, and rushed toward the front door, bounding out of it just as the bus started to pull away. He stood there on the side of the highway until the red taillights of the bus disappeared into the dark. It was another moment before the sound of the groaning engine faded away, leaving him with the still quiet of the night. Walking across the highway, he found the dirt road that led down toward the village of Nauzontla, about a thirty-minute walk away. Hesitating at the edge of the dirt road, he asked himself for the first time why he had gotten off the bus. He had never once thought of getting off . . . he had been returning to Jonotla . . . his family was expecting him . . . it was late . . . and dark . . . and how in the world would he ever get to Jonotla now? He had no answers, and so he set off down the road toward the village.

There was no moon in the sky. The darkness enveloped Celistino, so that he could see no more than a couple of feet in front of him. The road was rough and uneven, and at times he struggled to keep his balance. Soon the darkened shadows of the village loomed straight ahead, and shortly he walked on past the first buildings and a few dim figures on the street. He greeted them in a slightly disguised voice and hoped that no one would recognize him. For if they did, they would surely ask him why he was there, and he still had no answer. He had no idea why he had come or what he was going to do.

Most of the houses were dark inside, but whenever he passed a store whose brightly burning lantern cast its light out into the dark, he would carefully cross the street to avoid being too easily seen He knew some people in the village, and both he and his wife had relatives here.

He drifted quietly throughout the village, past the church, the plaza, the school, and countless houses. Everything seemed oddly familiar. Even though numerous changes had occurred since he had lived here as a boy, they were the sort of changes that came slowly and were sufficiently subtle not to have significantly altered the external appearance of the village. The buildings, the streets and paths, and even the trees and rocks seemed basically unaltered as they projected the darkened images of his boyhood years.

In a very real sense, he had not come to visit any of his relatives or friends, nor had he even come out of a desire to visit the village. He had come wholly to hold an internal meeting with himself, to compose a silent medley of fleeting memories from his past. It had been here, amidst all of this that was still so familiar, that his first dreams had been launched. His father's loss of his land over twenty years earlier had not only led to their move from Nauzontla to Jonotla, but had also provided the impetus to lay the first stone of the dream castle that had gradually developed in his mind into the elaborate structure that it was today.

After an hour or so, something told him that it was enough, and so he walked away from the village on the path that led through the mountains back to Jonotla. He did not think about the difficulty of making this trip on foot at night, a trip that even during the day was a rigorous five-hour walk. As he turned to get a last glimpse of the village of his birth, the familiarity which he had earlier sensed seemed to fade behind strange faces into the darkness.

The trail that connected the two villages ran up and down and across a series of high ridges. It began as a relatively indistinct footpath through open mountain fields and meadows. At other places, it was a clear-cut but narrow trail enclosed in a canopy of dense valley vegetation. At still other places, the trail narrowed, winding its way across steep mountain slopes. Celistino knew it well enough to proceed with studied caution, and he traveled even slower than usual because of the dark, stopping frequently to rest along the way.

The total darkness of the night created a kind of sensory deprivation for Celistino. His vision was severely diminished, and the stillness and quiet of the mountains—broken only by the occasional sound of a small animal scrambling through the bushes in fear of its unexpected visitor—brought a kind of ringing silence to his ears. Uncluttered by its usual external stimuli, his mind turned easily inward upon itself. The day ran rapidly and continuously through his thoughts: the *comandante's* visit, the money, the man who brought the "for sale" sign, the bus trip, the market in Zacapoaxtla, the old blind-and-deaf woman, Delfina, and Nauzontla.

There was a strange and complex intermingling of past, present, and future images in his mind, as there had been during the day. He had left at noon to visit the promised land, and at the same time to see Delfina and Gildardo, who resided not only in that dream of the future, but also very much in important memories of the past. He had spent a great deal of time discussing the past with Delfina, and at the same time attempting to mend the rupture that he had experienced between the reality of Delfina's present situation and what he had pictured it to be. And he had finally ended up, inexplicably, in Nauzontla. What had started out as a journey into the future had ended up as an excursion into the past at the village of his birth. It was all quite strange and yet somehow understandable, for the future has a peculiar tendency to become, suddenly and unexpectedly, the present, as the present becomes the past.

Celistino thought once again about the time that he and Delfina had been lost. He remembered that through it all he had never been frightened. It had been a game, an adventure, and he had never once doubted that if they couldn't find their way out, then his father would find them and lead them safely home. But things were different now. He felt lost again, and this time it was not an adventurous game, at least not since witnessing the weakening of his image of the promised land. Nor was his father around to lead him safely out. And he was less certain than ever about which path might lead home.

At daybreak he sat on a large rock at the northern edge of the ridge next to the one on which Jonotla was located. It had been a long day, a long night, and a long walk. As he sat there watching the village gradually appear on the distant mountainside, he seemed to be rebuilding that which only a few moments before had seemed hopelessly beyond repair. The village of Jonotla had, in many ways, been his first promised land, and the sight of it now suddenly renewed those visions of hope that had always sustained him. The changes that were occurring in the village provided just enough actual reinforcement to encourage further dreams, while the village was still sufficiently insulated from the absolute necessity for change to insure that dreams remained safely as dreams.

In a moment he would be back home with his family. Certainly, he told himself, there was a promised land out there somewhere, and he was sure that someday it would be his. Perhaps it lay eastward beyond the mountain peaks that cradled the morning sun, or westward into the Sierra, where the peaks level off into the great interior plateau. Or perhaps, just perhaps, it lay straight ahead in the village on the ridge beyond, which appeared as a series of contiguous shadows gradually illuminated by the same warm sunlight that touched his face and the world around him.

6–Good-bye, Ixoceolotl

The long, endless shadows of familiarity
follow tightly upon every step, the gods,
feared and respected in the safety of our
dreams. Good-byes to them are hard to
say, desertions of the self that they are.
But each good-bye echoes a new hello,
and, in the end, life flies into the sky on
little bird wings, a return to birth without
fear and without hope.

The mountain days grew longer and warmer, and the sun seemed larger and friendlier. Early in the morning, it gently nudged the chilled stillness of the night from its heavy sleep, slowly opening the empty blackness to the shapes and deep colors of life to which men were accustomed. Cradled in the arms of the intensely blue sky, it spread its warmth to the peaks and valleys of the mountains below, lingering a few moments longer each day in the company of its resurrected love—springtime. And when it finally left the sky, falling reluctantly behind the peaked horizon to the west, it splashed brilliant colors up into the evening, promises of yet another day to come.

The coffee trees had borne their harvest for one more year, and, for many people, that harvest was now translated into the cash that would in large part sustain them until the next season. For others, the source of life was still taking form beneath the soil, small capsules of tradition that provided both physical and spiritual sustenance. For almost everyone, it was a time of seasonal inactivity. A time to wait. For the corn. For next season. For a beginning. For an end.

A week had passed since Celistino's trip to Zacapoaxtla to visit Delfina. In that short time, he had worked hard at forgetting the most threatening parts of that experience. Although he had not worked during the week, he busied himself with tasks around the house, tending his pigs, repairing an old table, catching rats, talking with his wife and friends, and playing with his daughter. Not once had he looked at that sign fastened securely in the upstairs window. If he had seen it, he would have been reminded of the eventual sale of the house and consequently of Delfina and his trip. It was better not to remember.

Eudalia had questioned him about the trip, but he was unresponsive. Most of her questions had gone unanswered, and others unasked. Long ago, she had learned not to push Celistino for information that he was not ready to give. Once, when she had been particularly insistent, he had refused to speak to her for almost two weeks. Usually she found out all she wanted to know from him later in bits and pieces anyway. She could wait, too.

Despite his efforts, Celistino had not been able to forget entirely the events of the preceding week. Señor Rivera had returned. His anger had subsided, but he had still seemed puzzled and hurt, unable to understand why Celistino used the comandante in the way that he did. He told Celistino that the comandante had been insulting and had threatened him with jail, which was curious since the village didn't have one. Celistino felt guilty and angry with himself, but he did not know what to do about it. He thought for a second about returning the money, but he realized that Señor Rivera would undoubtedly refuse it. Instead, Celistino decided to buy Rivera a few drinks at don Luis' store. This decision seemed to be the right one, for they ended up having more than a few. They had departed that evening as friends, even going so far as to embrace one another, but although Celistino felt better about the incident, he was aware that Señor Rivera's apparent forgiveness might have been rooted solely in the alcohol rather than in any genuine feelings. But he would have to wait and see about that as well.

Shortly after his attempt to make amends with Señor Rivera, he had been visited by Juan Zaragoza, a man whom Celistino counted among his friends, although it was doubtful whether Zaragoza reciprocated the friendship. And if he had, he certainly didn't any longer.

He pounded heavily on Celistino's front door, and when Celistino opened it, he had angrily thrust the money that he owed straight into his chest. "Here is your money, all of it," he shouted. "Now, you no longer need to send your friend around looking for it." The phrase, "your friend," was filled with derision. "And let me tell you," Señor Zaragoza had continued, "if you continue to deal with me in this manner, then I will deal with you in the same way. Do you understand?" he asked menacingly. Celistino had quickly gestured that he understood. This was no time to be contrary.

After he left, Celistino cursed himself for leaving Señor Zaragoza on the list. He was a friend and his name should have been removed. And not only was he a friend, but he drank quite a bit and had a well-deserved reputation for physical aggression. He was strong and large as well. So all in all, Celistino realized that it had been a terrible mistake to have left him on the debtors' list. In fact, after these two encounters, he was increasingly aware that it had been a grave mistake to have left *anyone* on the list. There was no telling who would confront him tomorrow. And the high blue sky, bright sun, and longer days would do him no good at all; they would only make it that much more difficult to hide.

He had neither seen nor heard anything more from the *comandante* himself. That was, he hoped, a good sign, but he could not be sure. Perhaps the *comandante* had finished his collection efforts on his behalf or had given up for some reason, and the storm was really over. Or, perhaps, it was only a temporary lull, and the *comandante* would soon resume his attempts, angering more people and causing them to vent that anger at Celistino's doorstep. Celistino certainly didn't need that; he had more than enough unfriendliness. He might be able to continue to hide temporarily from those who pounded on his door, but there would be no easy way to avoid people on the street and in the stores. He could, of course, simply ignore the silent stares and cold shoulders from those named on his list, but he already felt more isolated and marginal than he could really bear. He could try somehow to mend his relationships, as he had with Señor Rivera. But he did not know how to accomplish this, and he would never be certain whether or not such efforts once made would be successful. He could never simply apologize and try to return the money, either. The money was not the point; everyone understood that it was rightfully his. The problem was solely in the way that he had gone about collecting the debts. And he did have to consider the damage to his reputation this event scored against the loss of dignity he would suffer from any subsequent attempts to apologize. In the world of the *mestizo* male there was no room for apology.

One course he could take involved that step which he had so often contemplated—leaving the village. Along with his varied dreams of commerce, it was one of the dominant themes of his dream book: the promised land. But his painful experience with Delfina was still too fresh in his mind; that dream had been temporarily shelved.

Whatever he might do, the time did not seem right just now. It was a time for waiting. Spring was coming, and there was absolutely nothing that one could do to hasten or slow its arrival.

Without really knowing why, Celistino set out for Ambroso's house. It was unusual simply to visit someone without a specific reason, even if everyone understood that the stated purpose was not at all the real one. It was a formality, but a relatively important one. As he walked the short distance, he sought an acceptable rationale for his visit. But none came, for it seemed that as soon as his mind came up with one possibility, it would rush on to the next. Each thought refused to be maintained long enough for him to make a decision about it. Before he knew it, he was standing in front of Ambroso's house, preparing to knock on the door.

Whatever explanation he would give Ambroso for his visit, they would both understand that the real reason was their friendship. As they struggled in their new *mestizo* world, true friends were not numerous, but those few they had were essential. They needed someone to trust in a world of threat and suspicion. It was not that the *mestizo* world was so *overtly* full of conflict, competition, and suspicion, but these attitudes were covertly present much of the time. It was as if one could never really be sure of anyone or anything. In such a world, true friendships did not develop easily, but once made they were binding, not so much because friends thereafter *had* to be friends, but because they wanted and needed to be friends.

Perhaps it was as essential for one's survival as was the need to eat. Both Celistino and Ambroso understood that, and so now Celistino found himself standing at his friend's doorstep, knowing in a sense why he was there, but still uncertain about what he was going to say.

He knocked on the wooden door. In a moment, the door opened several inches, and a wrinkled brown face peered out from the darkness inside. It was Ambroso's mother. Amidst the interior darkness and the deep color of her face and the jet blackness of her hair, the whites of her eyes stood out like small candles.

"Good morning, doña Evangelina," he said. "Is Ambroso here?"

She looked at him for what seemed like a very long time. Her eyes were somehow empty and yet so full. They slowly swelled with tears that clung there stubbornly, refusing to be fully released. "He is not here," she finally said with a firmness that was startling. It was a response which in certain undefinable ways carried so much more meaning than was present in the words themselves. Something was wrong.

Celistino felt a flash of panic. "Where is he?" he asked. "Is he working today? Or is he in the pool hall?" The questions came so fast that it seemed as if he didn't really want to hear the answers, but he couldn't continue to postpone the inevitable knowledge that would be his. And so he stopped and waited.

"He is not here," she repeated. She would not or could not say more. Celistino was certain that something was wrong now; why was she just standing there saying nothing? She was usually so much more friendly and talkative, even though in a rather formal way. But now she just repeated the same line, as if these memorized words somehow insulated her from the swell of feelings that lay behind her eyes. The same force that chained the tears to her eyes imprisoned her feelings—and her words—in her soul.

Celistino was about to start over again with the questions when he heard a man's voice from within. "Who is it, Evangelina? Is it Celistino?" the voice said softly. The old woman turned her face from the door and jerked her head upward in reply. "Let him come in. Don't make him wait outside," the voice continued. Celistino recognized the voice of Ambroso's father, although it was much slower and softer than usual. "Let him come in," he repeated. "He was Ambroso's friend."

Was? The word surrounded and weighed down upon Celistino. He felt increasingly empty and confused.

Ambroso's mother opened the door and motioned him to enter. His eyes took a moment to adjust to the darkness inside, for the one-room house had no windows and the back door was only slightly open. He was familiar with the sparsely furnished room. There were only a few chairs and a small table on one side of the room and a simply-fashioned wooden bed on the other. Ambroso had made the bed for his parents. They had always slept on straw mats on the floor, but as they grew older, Ambroso had insisted that their health and comfort required a bed. At first, they had discouraged the idea, but once the bed was made and they had adjusted to it, they seemed to enjoy it. Their son had moved increasingly away from their world, and, in a sense, the bed he made for them had been a peace offering to them, a gift from his new world into theirs in hopes of establishing a fragile link between them.

As Celestino's eyes grew accustomed to the dark, Ambroso's father gradually emerged from the back of the room, dressed in the traditional white that he had worn every day of his life since childhood. He was sitting in a straight-backed wooden chair with his hands folded across his lap. Doña Evangelina closed the front door, and the room became even darker. She walked silently over and picked up a chair, moving it close to the old man and motioning for Celistino to sit in it. She stood next to her husband, her bare feet planted firmly on the packed dirt floor. She wore a long white skirt and white blouse with red and gold embroidered flowers and designs across the top—traditional *indio* dress, which she, like her husband, had worn since she was a child. In fact, she was one of the few remaining women in the village who still periodically wore the traditional *indio quexquemitl*, a small decorated mantle, around her shoulders.

Celistino walked toward Ambroso's parents. Everything seemed to be moving in slow motion, including his thoughts. He sat down and waited to hear more.

"How have you been, Celistino?" the old man asked.

"Fine, very fine. And you, don Gonzalo?" Celistino replied. His voice sounded rushed.

"Ah, very well, as always. I hear that it was a very good year for coffee, that the trees were bending from the weight of the beans. That made it easier to pick from the highest branches." Don Gonzalo laughed, and Celistino smiled and nodded in agreement.

Typical house

But Celistino's smile masked a growing irritation. He had come for a simple visit with his friend, Ambroso, and since his first knock on the door he had been met with nothing but mystery. He still did not know where Ambroso was nor why his parents were acting so strangely. He only knew that he wasn't here. And what was all of this talk about coffee beans coming from don Gonzalo? Everyone already knew that it had been a good year; they had been talking about it for months. And people said the same things almost every year, unless it was really bad. And why should don Gonzalo talk about coffee anyway? He had always been a corn cultivator. Celistino was irritated, but he knew they had heard his question and would eventually answer it. They obviously had some reason for doing it their way.

"Well, that will please many people," don Gonzalo continued.

"What?" Celistino asked, still trying to understand precisely what was happening.

"The coffee, the coffee," the old man reminded him, disturbed that Celistino was not following his line of thought.

"Oh, yes, that's the truth." Celistino glanced around again as if to make sure that Ambroso was not present somewhere in the dark room.

"I do not have much land—no more than one hectare—and I plant only corn and beans, as I always have. It is not much, but it has been enough. It is enough, and it is not a lot of work to plant such a small piece of land. And I have always had my son." He paused and looked at his wife. "But I am getting old now, and it is getting harder. I must walk for more than half an hour each day to get down to my field, and even longer to get back up to the village. My back is bent and weak, and the digging and cutting is more

An indio campesino

difficult with each day that passes. The rocks in the ground seem to get bigger as I grow older. This I cannot change."

Celistino listened, still not at all sure of what was going on. There was a momentary silence, and he listened to that, too.

"But it's not a bad life, is it?" don Gonzalo finally asked.

Celistino did not know whether or not he wanted an answer, as he seemed to be talking more to himself than to anyone else. "No, it's not a bad life," he replied softly.

"But my son thought it was."

Once again, Celistino was startled by this use of the past tense, as if Ambroso had ceased to exist.

"And so he is gone," the father continued.

"Gone? Where?" Celistino asked.

"He left early this morning for Mexico City."

Celistino was stunned. Ambroso had mentioned nothing of his intentions to leave the village. They had often discussed the merits of such a move, but they had always agreed that, although the promised land assuredly awaited them, they would still wait for the proper moment before acting. Celistino had often envisioned his own departure without really thinking how he might feel about leaving Ambroso behind, but it had never occurred to him that Ambroso might move first and leave him behind. It was easier to envision his own departure and the attendant emotions that would be produced in others than it was to envision the departure of a real friend and the subsequent emotions that would be generated inside oneself. The unknown—overlaid with golden dreams—was more tolerable than loneliness.

The old man anticipated Celistino's next question. "He said that he was going to find work, that there was nothing here for him. Since he finished working on the road last August, there has been very little work for him." The old man shook his head. "Oh, there has been work, but not the right kind of work. He could have picked coffee beans, but he wanted something else; he could have stayed and helped me in the fields, but he wanted something else. And so he had to leave."

"Where will he work? Where will he stay?" Celistino asked.

"My wife's family has some relatives there that he can stay with, and he said that he has a job lined up in a factory owned by Señor Vasquez' nephew. I do not know what kind of factory it is."

Celistino knew. "They make things for bathrooms," he said. He noticed the vacant expression on don Gonzalo's face. "Toilets, faucets, sinks, pipes, and things like that," he tried to explain.

"I see," don Gonzalo said, although it was doubtful that he really did. No one in the village had a bathroom, and only the priest's house, the secondary school, and a couple of the wealthiest families had pressure flush toilets. Don Gonzalo had probably never even seen one in his entire life; it was as alien to his world as were automobiles, television, and electricity. And now, suddenly, the son he had always hoped would work alongside him in the cornfields in these mountains would be making toilets and sinks in Mexico City.

"Do you know, Celistino," the old man said, "that although Ambroso left this morning, he took the first step many years ago." He seemed to be trying to explain to himself how his son could have possibly leapt over that great cultural abyss. "It seems as if Ambroso was always dissatisfied, even as a little baby," he continued. "He would cry over the smallest things."

Ambroso's mother broke her long silence. "He was a good baby," she said, and her wrinkled face returned to its previous masklike rigidity.

"And then when he got to school it became worse," his father continued, ignoring the difference in opinion. "He got along well in school, but he became worse here at home. Sometimes he would not obey, and he was gone with his friends more and more."

"That is where it began—at school," doña Evangelina

added. "A little bit of school is all right—enough to learn
to read and to use numbers—but that is enough. After several years of school, one has learned enough of that. He
wanted to keep going to school, and so we let him. And
that is when it began."

Celistino was only half-listening. At least temporarily, he
had lost a friend. But even more unsettling was the realization that Ambroso had actualized one of their shared dreams.
They had discussed it and Celistino had written about it,
but now Ambroso had actually done it.

"He should have been in the fields with me instead of in
school," don Gonzalo went on. "I needed his help but, more
important, he needed to be learning the skills of a *campesino*. But he was always in school and he had other interests. I knew then already that he would not be a *campesino*. I could have stopped the school at any time, but I kept
hoping that it would make no difference and that even with
the schooling he would want to work with me in the fields.
But it was just not to be."

Celistino was busy sorting out his own thoughts, but he
still managed an acknowledging nod.

"And it ended because of that boy, Pepe," said doña
Evangelina. "That Pepe is mean and worthless; he talks
and drinks too much. He would not leave Ambroso alone;
he followed him everywhere—to the fields, the stores, the
pool hall, everywhere. Ambroso would come home sometime sad and quiet. Most of the time he would laugh and
talk, but whenever he saw Pepe, he would come home sad
and quiet. One day he came home from somewhere and
went out back and got his *machete*. It was late in the afternoon and so I knew that he was not going to the fields. He
was in that sad and quiet way, and so I asked him where
he was going. At first, he said nothing, but I asked again and
he said, 'To visit Pepe.' He was not mad—he never got
angry—but he was sad and quiet. I prayed all night until
he came home very late. He said nothing, but just went to
sleep."

Celistino nodded quietly again. He recalled the night that Ambroso had come to his house wearing his *machete*. Ambroso had seemed frightened of himself, and Celistino had given him refuge from that fear. They had talked for a long time, until they were both laughing and joking. Ambroso had left in a good mood, and Celistino had not thought about the evening again until this moment. It was clear to him now what had frightened Ambroso that night. He had thought it had probably been something that Pepe had said or done to Ambroso, but he now realized that it was what Ambroso had almost done to Pepe.

He realized that Ambroso's mother was probably right. They had often talked about leaving the village at just "the right moment," and until now, he had never really understood what either he or Ambroso had meant by "the right moment." It had always seemed to be a device to protect them from the necessity of facing a decision. But now he somehow understood. Ambroso's encounters with Pepe, increasing in intensity as they had, provided "the right moment." The rest—his childhood, school, his attitudes and feelings—were all prologue.

"He kissed us good-bye and promised to send us money every month," don Gonzalo said. "But I do not want money; I want my son back. This village is very sad, for all of its children are leaving."

Celistino wanted to help, but he did not know how. "He might come back," he said weakly. Neither of Ambroso's parents said anything, but Celistino could tell that they did not think that their son would ever return. There did not seem to be anything left to say or do, and so Celistino stood up to leave.

"Wait a minute," doña Evangelina said. "Ambroso told me to give this to you." She walked over to a small table, opened the drawer, and removed something from it. "Here," she said, handing him an object, "he said that he would not need this anymore, and he wanted it to be yours."

Celistino looked at the round gold medallion of *San

Martín de los Pobres that Ambroso had worn around his neck for the past several years. He folded his fingers around it and placed it carefully in his trouser pocket.

He said good-bye to Ambroso's parents and stepped out into the bright, sunlit street. As he walked slowly back to his house, his right hand holding the medallion in his front pocket, he recalled a conversation he had had with Ambroso the previous summer. The two of them had been working in Ambroso's father's field, and they had sat down to rest from the sun under a large tree that grew next to the path that led northeastward to the village of Ecatlán.

"Where does that path go?" Ambroso had asked.

"You know where that path goes," Celistino had replied. "To Ecatlán."

"And after that, where does it go?"

"You know that, too. It goes to Tuzamapan."

"And after Tuzamapan?"

"Well, you can go several ways, east and north."

"And after that?"

"I don't know," Celistino had stuttered in confusion.

"But it does go somewhere, right?" Ambroso had asked, still staring off down the path.

"Yes, it does go somewhere."

Now Ambroso was off down that path to somewhere, off to pursue an elusive dream, or perhaps, to flee a hopelessly shattered one. It was impossible to tell. Only one thing was certain: he was gone.

The distance from Ambroso's house to his own was not much more than fifty yards, but at the moment it seemed like miles. He approached the corner that was midway between the two houses still immersed in his thoughts of Ambroso and the promised land. Ambroso had only done what they both had so often talked about doing, but Celistino still felt somehow cheated. He hardly noticed the greeting of a young boy as he hurried past toward the plaza.

"It's going to be an important day, no?" the young boy added.

Laying the water pipes for the potable water system

"What do you mean?" Celistino stopped and asked.

"Don't you remember?" the boy shouted as he continued down the street. "Today is the dedication day for the new potable water system."

How could he have forgotten! Today was the culmination of over a year's work by scores of people. A large pump and filtering system had been installed at the upper end of the village, pipes had been laid under the main streets, and seven faucets from which villagers could draw clean water had been placed at convenient locations. It was the second major step in the development of the village to have been completed within the last year. The previous August had marked the completion of the road, and now just seven months later came the new water system. The next stage would be electricity.

And today was the formal dedication ceremony. The priest would be there, as would the government engineer who supervised the construction. There would be speeches and fireworks and music by the drum and bugle corps of the primary school. It would be an important day, indeed.

For just a moment, his thoughts returned to Ambroso. A series of questions ran through his mind. Why had he chosen to leave before such an important event? Why had he not waited one day? Didn't he realize what he was missing? No answers came; they were locked tightly in Ambroso's heart alone. Celistino's pace quickened as he hurried home to remind Eudalia and Avencia of the dedication ceremony, for they would all attend together. "What a day Ambroso is missing!" he whispered softly to himself.

Throwing open the front door of his house, he shouted for Eudalia and Avencia. His wife called from in back of the house.

"Hurry, hurry! Have you forgotten what day it is?" he shouted as he walked through the hallway and out the back door.

Eudalia was standing outside on the patio, putting the finishing touches on her long braided hair. She was wearing a white skirt with overlapping ruffles running from the waist to the hem. The front of her light blue, short-sleeved blouse was decorated with the same strips of lace. She had bought the skirt blouse and added the lace herself. It was a special outfit for special occasions; she had remembered the special nature of the day.

Celistino smiled when he saw her. He glanced at Avencia who was running around barefoot on the cement patio; she was wearing a clean blue dress covered with a layer of organza, and round white earrings. Like her mother, she was ready for the celebration.

Celistino dashed back into the house where he quickly removed his old black shoes and pulled on his newer ankle-high brown boots with the narrow white stripe running down the middle from ankle to toe. He would slip and slide a bit more on the cobblestones outside, but on special occasions, pragmatic considerations had to give way to proper demeanor. And then in another moment, they were walking together toward the plaza.

When they arrived, a crowd was already congregating around the old circular well that stood at the center of the plaza. Señor Valdez, one of the young schoolteachers, was assembling the fifteen-member white-clad drum and bugle corps in straight lines. The priest, in his very best clerical robes, was talking to the engineer who had supervised the work and several of the local government officials. They were all in good spirits, laughing and talking animatedly.

Eudalia and Avencia stopped to talk with several women who were standing on the edge of the plaza. Celistino walked closer to the center of the plaza near where the priest was talking with the others, thinking that he might overhear something important or interesting. As he walked, arms crossed over his chest, he almost bumped into a large man in his path.

Don Angel laughed. "You'd better watch where you are going," he said to Celistino. "You could get killed that way." And he laughed—a kind of grunt—again.

Celistino wished that there were some way he could start over again so that he could avoid this conversation. He still felt uncomfortable whenever he spoke to don Angel, and he would have preferred to have limited their contact to those situations where the content of conversations was more predictable, as in don Angel's store. There the conversation went: "Good afternoon, don Angel." "Good afternoon, Celistino. What do you need?" "A liter of kerosene, please." "Certainly, will there be anything more?" "No, that is all today. Thank you, don Angel." "My pleasure, Celistino." "Good-bye." "Good-bye." It was short, simple and controlled. Celistino did not want any more surprises from don Angel, and so he had always tried to control the circumstances in which they met. But this meeting was an accident, and he felt unprepared.

"This is a very important day," don Angel continued. "A very important day for all of us."

Celistino nodded his agreement silently.

"It is too bad that more people do not realize what you and I do," don Angel said, waving one hand around the plaza at fifty or so people who were standing around waiting for the big event to begin. "It is a disgrace that so few people are here. I thought that everyone in the village would be here—they should be. I think that the secretary of the *municipio*, or the priest, or someone should go and pound on every door to tell the people that they should be here." His face was scowling, and his pendulent jowls were vibrating. "But let them be ignorant," he concluded.

Celistino still said nothing.

"My wife says that she saw young Ambroso leaving early this morning on the bus," don Angel said, changing the subject. "He was carrying a large box, as if he might be leaving for a while. Do you know where he was going?"

"Yes," Celistino spoke his first words. "I know. He left for Mexico City."

"Really? Why?"

"To find work."

"Then he is gone for a long time, if not forever."

"Who knows?" Celistino looked away.

"It is probably better this way," don Angel laughed. "He and Pepe were really going after one another, and Ambroso was not doing too well. Something had to bend, and I guess it was Ambroso, that poor *pendejo*."

Celistino looked up at don Angel and stared directly into the eyes that he had for some time tried to avoid. For a long, endless moment he just stared. And then he turned his back on don Angel and walked away toward the other side of the plaza. For Celistino, it was an act of unparalleled bravery. He had always admired and tried to emulate this man; even after the incident in the pool hall he had somehow remained reverently afraid of him, refusing to fully deny his hero even after that hero had deserted him. But all of that was finished now.

Everyone in the plaza was ready. The young students in the drum and bugle corps stood in neat lines waiting for their schoolmaster to give them the cue to begin the ceremony. The priest, the engineer, and local government officials were assembled in front to lead the entourage up to the first water faucet to be dedicated. Next to the priest were seven men, each designated as a *padrino*, or godfather, for each of the seven new faucets. It was customary to select a *padrino*, and sometimes a *madrina*, or godmother, for new buildings or other village constructions. The positions were honorary. These seven men had bought *cohetes*, or rocket fireworks, for the celebration, and would have the honor of ceremoniously turning the faucets on as each was separately dedicated. Besides those who were to participate officially in the dedication, there were only about fifty villagers assembled.

The roll of the drums broke the relative quiet, and in a moment, the piercing blast of the bugles sounded a military-like reveille across the mountains. Led by the priest and the engineer, the group moved away from the plaza and up the shoulder of Tlaloctepetl toward the site of the first dedication. The crowd, joined by a few more people who had been attracted by the sound of the drums and bugles, followed behind. Celistino had rejoined his wife and daughter, and the three of them walked together on the fringe of the crowd.

Soon they all reached the first faucet located near the purification system, about one third of the way from the plaza up to the Chapel of the Little Virgin. The priest and the engineer stationed themselves near the faucet and turned to face the crowd. Celistino and his family moved under a large tree across the street from the dignitaries, making certain that don Angel was on the other side of the small crowd. The drum and bugle corps blasted another refrain, the signal for quiet. The bugles seemed to be playing at three different speeds, and one blared out a single note just a fraction of a second after all the others had finished. No one seemed to care.

The engineer stepped forward and addressed the crowd in a loud, dignified voice. "Ladies and gentlemen, young men and young women, children, you are the people of Jonotla; you are the people of the state of Puebla; you are the people of Mexico; you are the future," he began, his voice growing in emotional intensity as he went along. The crowd was silent; Celistino leaned against the tree. He wished Ambroso could be here.

The engineer proceeded to praise the cooperative effort of the state and local governments and applauded the virtues of hard work, dedication, patriotism, loyalty, and, most of all, progress. "Progress is the future of the hard-working people of Jonotla," he concluded to a round of cheers and whistles. It was a speech that he had, no doubt, given many times before; but it was something relatively new for the people of Jonotla.

As soon as he finished, the drum and bugle corps started playing again, simultaneously with the whistle and whine and explosion of the rockets as they soared overhead. The men in charge of the fireworks had a head start on the celebration, and they were already pleasantly drunk. They were having great fun, for it was not every day that one had the opportunity to send exploding rockets up against the sky. In their enthusiasm, however, they were somewhat careless with their aim, and several of the rockets zoomed and exploded just barely above the heads of the people, sending them running and laughing for cover.

As soon as things quieted down, the priest, who had retained a straight and serious face throughout, walked over to the faucet, bent down, and blessed it in the names of God the Father, the Son, and the Holy Spirit, and in conclusion splashed a few drops of holy water on the spigot. Just as he finished, another rocket whistled from its launching pad and landed in the large tree above Celistino's head, where it exploded, showering down leaves and twigs on the crowd below. The priest and engineer glanced at one another with a helpless look.

Once again, the drum and bugle corps started playing, and the first *padrino* stepped forward to release ceremoniously the very first drops of clean water for the people of Jonotla. The inaugural speech had been made; the faucet had been properly blessed; the rockets had soared and exploded in honor of the event. Now came the moment toward which all else had been moving. Celistino stretched his neck in order to glimpse that first drop of crystal-clear water. The *padrino* leaned over to turn the faucet, and everyone seemed to lean with him. But his first attempt at dislodging the handle to release the water was unsuccessful; it was stuck. He moved closer and gave it a hard twist, and the handle turned around several times, but no water flowed. He turned it again and again, until it would turn no further, and still there was not a single drop of water. The crowd was completely quiet. Shrugging his shoulders, the *padrino* walked over to the priest and the engineer, both of whom proceeded to the faucet and tried it themselves. But it was no use; there was no water.

They conferred with one another and decided to try the faucet in the plaza. The drum and bugle corps lined up again, and playing the same military march, led the procession back to the center of the village. The priest, the engineer, and the *padrinos* appeared grim and worried, whereas the faces in the crowd expressed bewilderment more than disappointment, and a gaiety that could not quite be suppressed by even the greatest failure.

In a moment, they were back at their starting point, and they assembled in proper ceremonial order once again. The engineer turned to the crowd and repeated his speech about dedication, hard work, and progress. "Progress is the future of the hard-working people of Jonolta," he concluded once again. It was the same theme as before; only this time the speech was much shorter. There were no fireworks to follow, for in their enthusiasm, the men had expended most of the rockets, and they were now saving the remainder for a sure thing.

Once again, the priest came forward and hurriedly blessed the faucet. The drum and bugle corps played, and the second *padrino* stepped up to the faucet to perform his designated duty. Everyone silently stretched to get a good view, but again there was nothing to see, for there still was no water.

A few groans of disappointment mixed with muffled laughter as the dignitaries conferred with one another about the increasingly embarrassing situation. Celistino watched silently, showing no signs of disappointment or amusement. Just a short hour before, he had been filled with excitement in anticipating this very event. And had he been told then that something would go wrong with the water system during the dedication, he would have predicted his own extreme disappointment. But now he felt nothing. It was as if something important had ended, and there had not yet been a new beginning.

The officials proceeded to a third site in search of a mere trickle of clear water. As the crowd left the plaza, two women in *indio* clothing were filling their large pottery vessels with water from the old well. They seemed to pay very little attention to the crowd as it moved away from the plaza. Their pots full, they secured them to their backs with tumplines strapped across their foreheads, and were soon on their way home.

This time there were no speeches or blessings or fireworks. The drum and bugle corps did start up again when they had all reached the third faucet, but the priest silenced them with a frown and a wave of his hand. There was no need for ceremony now. The engineer turned the faucet handle, but nothing happened. After consulting with the priest and several other men, he turned toward the waiting crowd and gave a short statement, explaining that there was air in the pipes and that the problem would be cleared up in a few days. With that, the men set off the remaining rockets amid a few shouts and cheers, and everyone went home.

The disappointment that might have been expected was not really in evidence, except in the faces of the priest, the engineer, and a few others. Only those who had visions, whether they were grounded in knowledge or in fantasy, of where this progress might lead had reason to be disappointed. For the rest, who approached this innovation with neither love nor hate, the temporary failure of the system was relatively meaningless. They accepted what happened, and went home with a simple shrug of their shoulders.

Surprisingly, Celistino walked casually with his wife and daughter toward the plaza with very little sign of emotion. "I wonder if the holy water was clean," Eudalia remarked as they walked along, covering her mouth with her hand to conceal her laughter, as well as her surprise over the fact that she had made such an irreverent remark. The laughter started slowly within Celistino, but it soon spread throughout his body, and did not finally leave until they had reached the plaza.

Several small children were busy trying to make the faucet in the plaza yield the promised water. They turned it, beat it with a stick, kicked it, and pushed it, but all to no avail. They rested for a moment, talking strategy among themselves, and then they once again went on the offensive, poking, prodding, pulling and punching, and failing once more where the fireworks, speeches, and blessings had also not succeeded. Seeing all of this, Eudalia and Celistino laughed even harder.

As they passed the plaza, Celistino looked to the street that ran steeply up the mountain toward the Chapel of the Little Virgin and don Chalo's house. Some interior voice now spoke softly, yet convincingly, to him. "You must go to see don Chalo," the voice said. It had happened to him many times before, but there was something different about the voice this time. In the past, he had always been drawn to don Chalo at times of relative disappointment, doubt, and despair. But now he was feeling comparatively happy and content, and yet, there was no mistaking the call of the voice.

He stopped abruptly at the edge of the plaza. Eudalia and Avencia did not notice and continued on for several yards. "Eudalia, wait," he called. She stopped and turned. "I believe that I will go to visit don Chalo," he said. "The poor man missed all of the excitement—he always does. And I know that he will enjoy hearing about everything that happened. The poor man is very lonely."

"Go on," Eudalia replied.

"I won't be gone long," he said, starting up the mountain.

The day was bright and warm, and Celistino pushed his hat down over his forehead to protect his face from the sun. His broad smile had its source in an inner calm and confidence, feelings that were so rare that he seemed to be especially savoring them. He was as certain as anyone can be about such things, that the positive feelings that he was experiencing were due to the fact that he had turned his back on don Angel.

Still painfully aware of the emptiness deep inside created by Ambroso's departure, he was nevertheless feeling somehow uplifted. At last, he had taken a stand by refusing to play by don Angel's rules. Ordinarily, his insides, his guts, his feelings, would have cried out, but his face and body would not have revealed what was twisting about beneath. "Yes, don Angel," he would have said. "You are right; things are better now that Ambroso—that poor *pendejo*—has left." And all the time his insides would have been screaming betrayal. But this time was different; he had experienced a unity of feelings and action to which he was not accustomed, and he was pleased with what he had experienced. The sorrow of Ambroso's departure was certainly now gone, but he had taken a stand, and it had been as much for Ambroso as for himself. He had previously been drawn to don Angel in pursuit of a dream created by the destruction of his past. And now the severing of those chains which tied his dreams, his life, to the person of don Angel was creating in him a sense of genuine freedom, in which he felt committed to the expectations of no individual or group. The frightening aspects of such freedom were not presently in his mind for he was like the escaped prisoner who has just had his first lung-filling breath of fresh air in years and has not yet had the time to worry about what he must do next.

He soon was passing the Chapel of the Little Virgin, and the deep valley to his left and the mountains beyond seemed especially beautiful to him. The greenery of the vegetation and the blue of the sky were both deep and true, while the distant sound of the rushing rivers below joined his heart in a quiet, joyful song.

By the time he reached don Chalo's house, his pace had quickened into a virtual skip and trot, and the song in his heart had been transformed into a windy half-whistle. He knocked loudly on the door; there was no response. Since the door was unlocked, he was certain that don Chalo was around somewhere. Pushing it open, he stepped inside and shouted a greeting. For a moment there was only silence, and then an undecipherable moan reached out from the area where don Chalo slept. The smile and the whistle disappeared as Celistino rushed to the small sleeping area that was partitioned off in one corner of the house.

He found don Chalo on his old, roughly fashioned bed wrapped in several blankets. He had propped himself up on his left elbow, and his right hand reached out in Celistino's direction, waving back and forth through the air as if it were crying out for something to hold. Some beads of sweat were poised on his forehead, and others ran down his face and down onto the bed. His graying hair was wet from the perspiration, and the smell of sickness was in the air.

Stepping forward, Celistino reached out and took don Chalo's hand in his; even though don Chalo was shivering violently, his hand was burning hot. His milky gray eyes stared at Celistino; they seemed to revolve in their sockets. His face produced a hesitant smile. "Is that you, Joaquina?" he asked softly. "I am happy that you are here." His face fought to maintain his smile against the force of his illness.

"Don Chalo, your wife is not here," Celistino replied. "She is dead. It is I, Celistino, your friend. You are very sick." His voice was choppy and his words uncertain; he was not sure what to say nor how to say it.

Don Chalo lowered himself back on the bed, and with his left hand, he reached beneath the blankets and pulled a small silver cross to his chest. He smiled again. "Thank you for coming, Joaquina. Thank you for coming," he said. "I have great faith, but I am still afraid. We will go together, and you can show me the way."

Celistino reached over and felt his forehead. Like his hand, it was fiery hot. He lowered don Chalo's right hand to the bed, releasing it, and pulled the blankets up over his shoulders. But don Chalo protested. "No, Joaquina, take my hand, take my hand. I need your help, for I still cannot see. Soon my vision will be restored, but for now I need you to show me the way." His pleading voice was full of desperation, so Celistino once again held his hand.

Celistino's eyes focused on don Chalo's old, worn, and bony hand that tightly clutched the small, silver cross to his chest. He was reminded of his own father's death and the unfathomable experience that he had had as a twelve-year-old viewing his father's lifeless body. A sense of *déjà vu* rushed through him: the same worn hand clutched the same small cross. Feeling uneasy, he thought for a moment of leaving and getting a neighbor to care for don Chalo. But the image of his father held him there. For years, he had felt guilty about his father's death, as if he were partly responsible. His father had felt deserted when he lost his land and the way of life he valued, and, in his own life, Celistino had further deserted him by moving further and further from his past. He realized that he and his father were different men living in different times, and that he should feel no remorse over that fact. And, yet, there was something that would not quite release his soul from the past; being there with don Chalo and his memories of his father's death made him once again aware of this.

He decided not to leave. If help came, it would come. If death came, it would come. But he would not leave; he would remain by don Chalo's side. "Don't worry, old man," he whispered, "I am here."

"Is it time to go?" don Chalo asked.

"No, not yet," Celistino answered slowly.

"Good, good, I must go visit the Little Virgin before I leave. I have visited Her almost every day for many years, and I must not miss visiting Her on my last day." He made no physical effort to move, although it was impossible to know where his mind was traveling. "I know that I will soon be with her in the heavens," he continued. "But this is different; it is my last chance to visit Her as ...," and there was a long pause before he completed the sentence, "... as a man."

"Don Chalo, you will have many chances to visit the Chapel," Celistino said. "You are going to get better, I know. The Virgin Mother in heaven will wait for you, but the Little Virgin of the sacred rock will see you for many more years. You are going to get better, I know."

Don Chalo did not seem to hear. "Is everything ready, Joaquina?" he asked. His head was turning rapidly from side to side, and he was becoming more and more difficult to understand. "The candles, do you have the candles? And the flowers, too, the wild flowers, are they here? I am beginning to see, I am beginning to see, Joaquina. . . . Where are the candles? I have the cross, but where are the candles? I need the candles to see, to see, to see . . . ," and his words tapered off along with the movement of his head until he was completely still and quiet.

"Don Chalo, don Chalo," Celistino whispered, "are you all right?" He threw the blankets back and could see that he was still breathing. He covered him up again and stumbled back into the cooking area. If he could get something warm into don Chalo's body, it might somehow help. After a moment of searching, all that he could find was a jar half full of *pulque*. The coals in the hearth were still live, and Celistino added a few sticks until he had a small fire. He poured the *pulque* into a small pan and placed it over the fire. After it was good and warm, he filled a cup with the steaming liquid, and, remembering the magical effect that the concoction had a few months earlier on him and don Chalo, stirred in several spoonfuls of honey.

He rushed back to the bed and propped don Chalo up against his shoulder. "Here, don Chalo, drink this. Drink this," he ordered as he tried to force don Chalo's mouth open with one hand. The first bit of the drink ran out of the corners of his mouth, but in another moment don Chalo was swallowing the *pulque* and honey just as quickly as Celistino could pour it. His eyes never opened, but Celistino felt encouraged by don Chalo's willingness to drink the brew. When the cup was empty, Celistino eased the old man back into the bed and pulled the blankets up around his neck. The chills had stopped, and his breathing seemed more relaxed and normal. It would be best for him to sleep.

Celistino walked back into the cooking area and poured himself a small shot of *pulque* which he downed with one gulp. He returned to the bed and sat down in a chair next to don Chalo and waited. Don Chalo was no longer restless although he mumbled incomprehensibly during his sleep, which lasted for several hours.

When he finally woke, his eyes opened slowly and blinked away the sleep. "How do you feel, don Chalo?" Celistino asked, rising from his chair and reaching over to feel the old man's forehead. The fever had broken.

"Who is it?" don Chalo asked.

"It is I, Celistino," he said, hoping that this time don Chalo would recognize him.

"Ah, Celistino, my friend. What are you doing here? I was sleeping and did not hear you come in."

"You are sick, don Chalo, and you were dreaming. You had a very high fever, and you were talking. I have been here for a long time."

Don Chalo looked puzzled. "What did I dream, what did I say?" he asked.

"Oh, lots of different things, crazy things. You thought that I was . . . I was someone else."

"Who?"

"I don't know, just someone else," Celistino lied. He was reluctant to mention don Chalo's wife, being afraid that it would only upset him, especially if he mentioned that he had been so certain that he was going to die. But even though he refused to tell him, it seemed that don Chalo knew who he had imagined Celistino to be.

"Do you know what is wrong with you, don Chalo? Perhaps, if you tell me about it, I can get some medicine from the schoolteacher."

Don Chalo laughed. "Do they have medicine for old age?" he asked. "It may have been the winds that carried the sickness, and it may have been the cracks in the walls that let it into my house, but it is my old age which let it into my body."

Celistino laughed without really knowing whether don Chalo wanted him to do so. He had been taken by surprise by don Chalo's response, and, therefore, he was unsure how to react himself.

"The one truth, Celistino, is that I am an old man. Whatever else might be true, that one fact cannot be denied. And an old man is tired."

"But when you are not sick," Celistino protested, "you are always so lively and alert. I never thought of you as tired before."

"That is only because I do not wish to burden anyone else with my age or my fatigue. I am an old, tired man who has covered my body, my age, with new clothes. But I have no more new clothes—they are old and worn-out just as I am. So, to you I am not tired, but inside I have been tired a long time. And when clothes reach a certain age, worn and ripped, they become useless and must be discarded."

Celistino laughed again, but it was obvious that don Chalo was not making jokes. "But, don Chalo, you are not a bunch of old clothes," he said. "You are a man, and you are alive."

"You have only half the truth," don Chalo said. "I am old and tired, and as a result I am only half a man and half alive."

"No, no, no," Celistino protested. It did not occur to him, but for perhaps the very first time he was defending don Chalo, and the fact that he was unaware of that defense meant that it was genuine, coming from his heart rather than his mind.

"When does spring arrive?" don Chalo asked.

"I don't know," Celistino replied. "Perhaps, in a few weeks or a month."

"I always looked forward to the coming of spring. It is a time of great happiness. But this year I will be gone before it arrives. It will come and find me in the ground in *la tierra del campo santo*.* I will miss that."

"Don Chalo, you are not going to *la tierra del campo santo*," Celistino interrupted. "You are going to get better." He sounded more convinced than he actually was, for don Chalo still did not look at all well.

"It is not that I am afraid of dying," don Chalo continued, ignoring Celistino's optimism, "but I only wish that I could see spring once again. Then I would go willingly."

Celistino noticed that don Chalo used the word "see" even though he was totally blind. He did not understand what don Chalo meant; perhaps, he still was confused from his high fever; perhaps, it was only a manner of speaking.

---

* Consecrated ground, the cemetery

"I am not afraid of dying," don Chalo repeated, as if he was trying to convince himself. "God would like to punish us for our many sins, but Our Lady will not allow it. She is Our Mother, Our Protector, and She has compassion for Her children. And I know the Little Virgin in a very special way," he said, pointing in the direction of Her chapel. "I talked to Her every day, and She will recognize me when I come. She will take care of me, as she always has. If She will only let me remain so that I can see spring." His face was brightening, and he did not seem so tired nor so old.

Celistino started to ask don Chalo about the symptoms of his illness again, but before he could finish his sentence, don Chalo interrupted him. "That is enough about me," he said. "What about you?"

"What do you mean?" Celistino asked.

"You are still young, fully alive, fully a man. What about you?"

"I still do not understand."

"I mean, what do you see today? Almost every time you come to visit, you talk about new places, new things, and big changes. What have you got for me today?" His small smile was one of great expectation.

Celistino was so surprised by all of this, he was unable to respond immediately. He had always assumed that don Chalo did not like to hear about his various visions of the future, and he had persisted in these discussions only because he felt they were for don Chalo's own good. But now, for the first time, don Chalo seemed to be encouraging him.

"Well, don Chalo, they did dedicate the potable water system today," Celistino finally answered. "And I believe that it is an important part of our progress." He made the sounds, but they were hollow, without meaning and without exuberance. In the past, don Chalo had always been indifferent or antagonistic toward his views of progress, and when Celistino presented his ideas, he had always done so with considerable enthusiasm. But now that don Chalo seemed to be a sympathetic and willing listener, he had some-how lost this enthusiasm. It was a contradiction that could be explained only if it was understood that Celistino's visits were more for himself than they were for don Chalo.

Celistino's ideas would always be safeguarded as dreams as long as they had the living conflict with the past in the person of someone like don Chalo. As long as there was someone, other than himself, who remained to be convinced of the validity of his visions of the future, the good life, and progress, then those visions could comfortably continue as words, as dreams. But once they lost that support, even if only temporarily, then they could no longer be sustained in the same way, for the only argument left, then, was with himself. Celistino had attempted to protect himself when-ever his dreams were threatened by reality by creating con-versational conflicts with don Chalo, believing these en-counters to be the essential conflict that he was attempting to resolve and thereby avoiding the more painful and dif-ficult task of resolving the conflict between *his* past and *his* present.

He was beginning vaguely to understand all this, although he was as yet uncertain as to where it would leave him. So much had happened in one day.

"Celistino, I want to tell you something," don Chalo said. "I am always talking about life as it used to be, because that life is locked tightly within my soul. It was a good life, and if things have to be different, then I am sad. That is the truth; it is my way. But my way is not your way. What is locked tightly within my soul is different from that which is locked within yours. And only God knows which is right."

Celistino nodded his head, and old don Chalo smiled and closed his eyes and fell asleep once again. He sat there until he was certain that don Chalo was not going to awaken, and then he got up and walked quietly out the door. He was certain that don Chalo was much improved, and he planned to return in the morning to make sure.

The day was still pleasantly warm, and the cloudless sky

invited the continued warmth of March. Celistino walked slowly down the path leading to the center of the village and home. His quiet mood contrasted vividly with the mood with which he had approached don Chalo's house several hours earlier. A lot had happened to the world of Celistino de la Cruz that day. In a way, the three main pillars of support which had for so long sustained him in a difficult world, in the crack between past and future, had been destroyed, or at least, transformed.

He had turned his back on the man who had for so long represented what he had imagined his ideal future to be: don Angel, the store owner; don Angel, the businessman; don Angel, the traveler; don Angel, the innovator; don Angel, the respected; don Angel, the consulted. This didn't mean that he had turned his back on those goals which were valued in his dreams; he would still strive to get away from working in someone else's mud. Nor did it mean that he had cut himself off entirely from don Angel; that would be impossible in such a small community. He would continue to see don Angel in necessary formal settings and, perhaps, in less formal ones as well. It was conceivable that he would even venture into the pool hall once again. But the goals within his dreams would never again be tied to don Angel. He would have no hero; he would have only himself.

Ambroso, his best friend, had also left on this day. The void would be difficult to fill, but there would be other close friends. In the meantime, he would have to be his own refuge.

And lastly, something which he still did not fully understand had happened at don Chalo's house. The imagined conflict that he had created between himself and don Chalo had dissolved into the internal conflict that it really was. Again, he was left with nothing but himself. He would return to visit don Chalo, but never for quite the same reason. And as the day of spring's arrival grew closer, don Chalo would seem to draw strength from its inevitable coming. For him, a blind man, to see spring was the only incentive that gave him life. As always, spring did come, and don Chalo *saw* it.

There had been a lot of good-byes today, and, as a consequence, one part of Celistino felt confidence while the other felt despair. It was the nature of his circumstance, torn from the past and not yet in the future and uncertain where he would place himself even if he could freely choose, that he should simultaneously experience pessimism and despair, as well as optimism, hope, and victory.

As he passed the Chapel of the Little Virgin and the sacred rock of Tlaloctepetl, he stopped to gaze out over the mountains. The late afternoon shadows were cast over the valley below, and the orderly formation of night-flying birds, carried on the swift wind currents, weaved in flight several hundred feet below where he stood. In the stillness Celistino could hear an old truck loaded with beer and soft drinks noisily make its way up the steep, winding, bumpy road, its old engine straining to make the final climb up the shoulder of Tlaloctepetl. Celistino looked down several hundred feet into the valley and watched the truck. Its engine was overheated, and for a moment he doubted whether it would survive the assault on this ancient mountain. But somehow after a long, doubtful moment the truck made it, and he watched until it disappeared around the curving road leading into the village.

Turning away from the valley, he continued his walk toward home where he would spend the evening with his family. But the day had somehow changed him, although he was uncertain exactly in what way. He would think about that tomorrow or the next day; now, it was sufficient for him just to feel the way he did without understanding it fully. Soon the sun would glide behind the mountain to the west, and the quiet darkness would envelop the village. He would yawn, stretch, and get a good night's sleep. Tomorrow, the beaming sun would once again open the village to the day, as familiar shadows would creep slowly across the face of the land. But those same shadows would appear somehow changed—darker or lighter, larger or smaller, straighter or more angled. Everything was different. The shadows cast by others, and most of all, by himself would seem less fixed, without the same hopes and fears—the parents of his dreams—to support them. In only two years he and his family would be gone from the village, most likely forever. He seemed to know that now. Like a butterfly shedding its cocoon, a part of him was gone forever and another part had just replaced it. And only the laughing sun knew whether it was all for the best or for the worst, whether it was simply the dawn of a new day, or the dusk of the final eve.

7-Lost Memories

Just yesterday, it was there before my eyes
and inside my heart. Now, it is already a
dreamtime long ago.

In 1973, the remodeling of the old plaza that had started three years earlier was completed. The patchy grass and the dirt that always turned to mud by the frequent rain, both familiar sights in the plaza, were now completely covered by cement. The trees had been removed and replaced by neat stone flower boxes graced with carefully selected flowering plants. The crumbling cement benches were gone, leaving no place to sit and pass the day. The circular well in the center was still the same, although it had been cleaned and scrubbed to remove the black and green fungus that had collected over the years. Even the decaying statue of Benito Juárez had been removed and destroyed; one of the flower boxes occupied the position from which he had for so long looked out over the plaza, and the village activities which were centered here.

Other changes had arrived. Buses and taxis now entered the village on regular schedules, their path smoothed by a paved street leading up from the lower end of the village into and around the plaza. After forty years, the Chapel of the Little Virgin was finally being finished. A high vaulted roof of cement was being constructed, and the floor completed to enlarge the space for worshipers. Perhaps, most significantly, Celistino's bright star in the sky—electricity— had arrived, and sundown would never quite be the same again.

It seemed that many of the things that Celistino had dreamed about and recorded faithfully in his notebook were now reality. They were no longer only daydreams, played out in his notebook, or his conversations with don Chalo; they were out there for everyone to see.

Everyone except Celistino. For in the midst of all of these changes which he had for so long enthusiastically supported in his dreams, Celistino had left the village of Jonotla. He was gone forever. He left to find work, he told friends. He and his family had gone to Tetella de Ocampo for a while, but they had soon moved on. No one seemed to know exactly where. To Papantla or Poza Rica, some said. To Peubla or Mexico City, thought others. One friend even said that he had heard that Celistino had gone to the United States, but that it was probably only to Tezuitlan or Vera Cruz. But he had left, and the dreams that had insulated him were now memories in the lives of those that

The plaza

knew him. Like his friend Ambroso, he said that he left to find a job, to realize a dream. No one could know the truth of that statement. But if there were any truth to it at all, it was equally true that he had left because of a broken dream and, perhaps, in hope of resurrecting that dream in a new place under different circumstances.

Coincidentally, a few months after Celistino left, don Angel suddenly died. Don Angel's wife, doña Josefina, buried him in *la tierra del campo santo*, an honor which even don Angel richly deserved. She closed down the pool hall, but she continued to operate the store. She never had agreed with him on the whole matter of the pool hall, feeling that it somehow represented the evil forces of the universe. Although she never spoke out publically against don Angel's pool-hall business, at just the appropriate time her penetrating eyes would convey disdain for the whole enterprise. So upon her husband's death, she sold the tables and locked the doors forever on that testing ground for village manhood.

A few months after don Angel's funeral, don Chalo died as he had lived for the past few years—alone. He, too, was buried in *la tierra del campo santo*. He had gone at last to rejoin his wife and those memories with which he had lived. The rusty nails from which he used to hang his meager wares at the bottom of the steps leading to the Chapel of the Little Virgin were still there. Few would notice them now, and if they did, they would see them as rusty nails, nothing more. Still they were small and simple reminders of such important memories. They were the only visible part of don Chalo's legacy, and they would always have a lot to say to those who cared to remember.

The small world of Jonotla had changed so much in so short a time. Those, like Celistino, who were blessed, or cursed, with life moved unavoidably toward other worlds, improvising the script as they went, although it seemed that the basic structure of their world was preordained and the final act written. Others, like don Angel and don Chalo, were written out of the script altogether. So far apart in life, they now lay only fifty feet from each other, their lives fading slowing into the chasm of lost memories.

Like a surging flash flood, the changes will continue to come. And the lives of the villagers will continue to speak to those changes. Some of them will continue soundly to applaud the changes that are taking place as symptoms of a much needed improvement in the standard of living. The expanding coffee industry and other commercial growth, they will argue, will create better wages and a general improvement in the quality of life. They see themselves as a small part of progress, noting that there is no sense in denying them the right to what much of the world already has or is working toward. Others, through their behavior or their despair, will continue to condemn the changes as the destruction of a viable and rewarding cultural system which has an equal right to maintain itself. Their lives point to the generally unaggressive, noncompetitive harmonic world view of the *indio* as something of immense value to be maintained, noting that, as far as progress goes, there is nothing to be gained in the long run by tying one's rowboat up to the *Titanic*. Still others will point out that any change entails both gains and losses, and that before one can fully understand the extent and nature of the one, he must comprehend the extent and nature of the other.

Celistino and the two men who had been to some extent the living representatives of both his dreams and his memories are all gone from the village. Celistino no longer sits quietly in his room, surrounded by that green mountain stillness, studying his illustrated dictionary. Don Chalo will never again sell his wares at the bottom of the chapel steps, reminiscing alone with his past. And don Angel will never again place his huge frame in a chair at the back of the pool hall and shake uncontrollably with laughter. All of that is over. But the village of Jonotla remains. Others will continue to struggle and search there. But these three men, their lives, and the village that they knew are already dim memories fading into the mountain haze.

Appendix: Anthropology and Human Life

One bright November morning I went to visit don Chalo, who was in his usual post at the bottom of the steps leading to the Chapel of the Little Virgin. It was one of those days when the air was so still and life so quiet that the surrounding mountains seemed quite unreal, like a painted backdrop for some movie. We talked for a while about the usual things—the weather, crops, and local gossip—and filled the gaps in our conversation with long moments of silence. After one such conversational lull, don Chalo suggested that we go up into the chapel. He gave no explanation, and so I dutifully followed him up the stairs, which he climbed with the speed and assurance of a much younger, sighted person. We sat alone together on the small bench at the back of the chapel. Our silence magnified the stillness that was all about us. Don Chalo's face pointed downward, his head cupped between his rough hands. As was so often the case, he seemed to be in his own world. Suddenly, without looking up, he said, "Tell me what you see."

At first I did not understand, and sensing my hesitation, he added, "Here in the chapel. Tell me what you see." Looking around the mostly bare chapel, I started to describe what I saw—the altar, the crepe-paper decorations, the candles, the flowers, and finally the Little Virgin encased in the middle of it all. As I talked, I thought of his blindness and my sight and all that he was missing. I tried to be as detailed as possible, for I felt an obligation to somehow create vivid images in his mind. He didn't move, but occasionally he would grunt or mumble inaudible sounds that made me feel that I was accomplishing what I had set out to do.

Finally I ran out of words, and I sat silently scanning the chapel for important elements that I had overlooked. Satisfied that I had done a more than adequate job, I turned to don Chalo, who had still not moved, and said, "That is all. There is nothing more of importance that I can see."

He remained quiet for a moment more, and as he moved his head toward mine, he smiled and said, "Very good, very good. But you see nothing more? Are you certain?" His smile changed rapidly into a puzzled and bewildered expression.

I again gazed at the chapel, looking in desperation for something of importance. I quickly reviewed what I had described—there was nothing of real significance left. I couldn't describe every crack in the wall or spot on the floor. I wanted to please the old man, but I could find nothing more to describe. "What else is there?" I finally asked.

He stood up, grunted to himself, and walked toward the door. Now the puzzled look was on my face. I followed him outside into the sunlight. As we walked down from the chapel, settling down once more on the last step, I again asked, "What else is there, don Chalo?"

"I don't know." He spoke softly and slowly. "What you said was good. I remembered many things. But you did not tell me everything." I protested that I had tried, but that such a task was quite impossible, and I again asked to know what I had omitted.

"I don't know. But everything that you described was outside of you while nothing came from inside. Did you not see anything here?" He jabbed his finger against his chest and became quiet once again.

Immediately, I knew what he meant. I had not known him very long, but he repeated the same gestures and expressions so frequently that they were difficult to misunderstand. He had said the same thing to Celistino and used the same gesture only a few weeks earlier when discussing the future of the village. Then, as now, he was emphasizing the importance of his inner feelings and memories. Perhaps because of his blindness, or perhaps only because he was the person he was, don Chalo's inner feelings were especially important to his comprehension of the world. My description of the chapel had been outwardly detailed and accurate, but it had lacked any depth of feeling and emotion. Actually, I always had rather strange and strong feelings when I was in the chapel. It was so still and quiet with an almost surrealistic quality about it. This time had been no different. Yet, I had omitted these feelings entirely from my description. In my attempts to be accurate, I had sanitized my description for don Chalo, cleansing it of all emotion and mystery. At first, I had been reasonably satisfied with it, but he hadn't been, and now neither was I.

I soon excused myself and walked back to our house, where I hid for the next few days, reviewing my field notes and census data. Don Chalo's comments had disturbed me greatly. This disturbance stemmed from something much deeper than simply a sense that I had somehow failed to please an old, blind friend. His comments seemed instead to question the very heart of what I was doing in the village, collecting lifeless data and information. As a result, although I continued in my planned research, I started to pay closer attention to the human plot that was unfolding all around me.

Actually, don Chalo had raised two questions that have plagued the social sciences ever since their birth: What is objectivity? and, depending upon the response to that question, How is it best achieved in understanding and presenting material about human beings? Historically, there have been many responses to these questions, and there continue to be diverse answers even today. A review of the various solutions that have been offered by important thinkers in social science would serve no purpose here, as such reviews are commonplace in the many survey texts dealing with the historical development of theory in the various social sciences. Instead, I wish only briefly to elaborate on the meaning of don Chalo's comments for social science and how what he said is related to this book.

Despite a certain degree of latitude in modern social science with regard to the question of objectivity, as well as with numerous related questions, there is a single idea that increasingly underlies much contemporary research. This is the idea that many of the basic faculties possessed by human beings are liabilities when carrying out research and therefore must be purged from both the researcher and his subjects. Standardized, replicable methods are viewed as necessary in order to create a barrier between the emotions and feelings of the researcher and the social world that he is trying to understand. This is seen as objective data collection. Equally, research must be reported in such a way that the emotions and feelings of the subjects are either absented entirely as irrelevant, or are diluted into lifeless forms, structures, processes, or simple statistics. This is viewed as objective reporting. With such a perspective, the description that don Chalo desired would have to be relegated to the status of "mere" subjectivity.

Now, few would deny that it is desirable for the researcher to attempt to understand human phenomena as accurately as possible. But the real question raised by don Chalo, and, in part, this book, is whether the removal of feeling and emotion from research and reporting of that research is, in fact, objective. For if objective methods are those which are most appropriate for the particular phenomenon under investigation, and if objective reporting is that which most accurately conveys to the reader the phenomenon studied, then the complete removal of feeling, emotion, and passion from social-science research and writing must be seriously questioned. Human experience is constituted of more than the external, conscious, rational, observable, and physical; there is also the internal, unconscious, irrational, intuitive, and psychical realms. Humans do more than answer questions on a survey instrument; they live, and they do so not only by following norms and adhering to values, but by bringing a special passion to their experience. Thus, being an important part of the human experience, passion has an objective place in both social-science research and writing. Otherwise, a considerable part of the human experience— joy, hope, fear, love, freedom, sorrow, despair, absurdity, and countless other emotions—is irrevocably diluted into explicit relationships among measurable variables. Otherwise, the researcher becomes little more than a trained technician plodding through predetermined routines as any successful machine might hope to do. And, otherwise, the subjects of research become little more than mechanical artifacts functioning in unison to the tune of structures, functions, and processes. Human life is passionate, and in order to be wholly understood and conveyed, it must be partly researched and presented with passion.

Among the several social sciences, anthropology has most often remained open to diverse methods of research and writing, and there has always been a home for what the anthropologist Jules Henry called "anthropology with plot." Perhaps it is in the nature of anthropological field work that we anthropologists come to think of our research largely in terms of individuals and emotions rather than faceless abstractions and generalizations. The field is a home, if only for a year or so, and the individuals with whom one shares that small slice of life whose passion is so accentuated by the problems of psychological, cultural, and physical adaptation remain securely and warmly in our memory. It is precisely that human dialogue between the anthropologist-human and the informant-human that provides anthropology with its greatest strength and its vital life. And no matter how much anthropologists write in terms of generalizations, patterns, functions, and structures, the human faces refuse to disappear, if not from our writing, then from our memory. Thus, our research has not generally been limited by the usual academic fortresses constructed out of normative terminology, methodology, and other facets of discipline maintenance; instead, it has always been ultimately bounded by the limits, whatever they might be, of the question, Who is humankind? The question now facing anthropology is how long, in the face of increasing pressure toward a unidimensional science which denies a place for passionate ethnography, can the eclecticism of anthropology be maintained? Somehow, the answer to that question must be found in our own lives, in our ability and willingness to see ourselves as necessary for the understanding of other lives.

Several weeks after I returned to Washington, D.C., from Jonotla, I went alone to the National Shrine of the Immaculate Conception to fulfill a promise that I had made several months earlier to don Chalo. We had been sitting together in his old house, talking, the evening sun behind the mountain to the west, when he pulled a candle from the small bag draped over his chair. He began to talk about his wife and his own eventual death, and he asked me to take the candle to the "grand cathedral" in Washington that I had described to him once before. He had no real idea what Washington was like or even where it was, and his image of the shrine was constructed solely from my limited description. Yet every time he mentioned it, his face seemed to shine until he grinned and shook his head at the vision that illuminated his darkness. That day was no different. Through his wide smile, he said that surely such a grand cathedral was powerful and that he wanted to make sure that God and the Virgin were aware of him. The gift of the candle was to help insure that. And then he turned to me, and saying that it was important that friends remember each other as well, he gave me a knife with an eagle-head handle.

As I went into one of the several alcoves in the basement chapel at the Shrine, that evening with don Chalo seemed to be right before my eyes. I was still in that period of adjustment that anthropologists characteristically experience after field work as they work through the cultural-psychological lag of returning "home". At times, I would hear a faint sound or briefly whiff a familiar smell and find myself momentarily returned to Jonotla. As I placed the candle on a small stand alongside some others, the stillness around me transported me back. The candles flickering in front of me —don Chalo's now among them—blurred and appeared for a moment to be in the Chapel of the Little Virgin, there in the shadow of Tlaloc. The swell of emotion that I felt as I thought of don Chalo and the others in Jonotla—the hope, sorrow, joy, and absurdity of their lives—surrounded me until I could hardly breathe. After almost an hour of intense memory, I left with a firmer conviction than ever that the sort of feelings that I had just experienced, as well as those that don Chalo expressed when he asked for this small favor, are at the heart of our understanding of other people. How foolish we are to view this surge of life that we experience in ourselves and others as irrelevant and even dangerous to our research, smothering it in a fog of terminology, tables, and statistics. Don Chalo knew that it was foolish. To deny a place for human passion in social science is to deny a part of our own, as well as all others', humanity. We are in pursuit of an elusive morning star—humankind—and to measure and chart its course without also attempting to document and understand the passion of its journey is hopeless. I can only hope that in a small way this book contributes to such an understanding and that it lives up to the expectations of don Chalo when he asked me to describe that incredible chapel from both my mind and my heart.